New perspectives in continuing education and training in the European Community — Seminar report

CEDEFOP

Report of a seminar
held in Berlin on 14-17 October 1980
organized jointly by CEDEFOP—European Centre for the
Development of Vocational Training and the Commission
of the European Communities

Published by:
European Centre for the Development of Vocational
Training
(CEDEFOP),
Bundesallee 22, D-1000 Berlin 15, Tel. (030) 88 10 61

The Centre was established by Regulation (EEC)
No 337/75 of the Council of the European Communities.

This publication is also available in the following languages :

DE ISBN 92-825-3534-7
FR ISBN 92-825-3477-4
IT ISBN 92-825-3536-3

Cataloguing data can be found at the end of this publication

Luxembourg : Office for Official Publications of the European Communities, 1983

ISBN 92-825-3535-5

Catalogue number : HX-32-81-956-EN-C

Reproduction in whole or in part of the contents of this publication is authorized, provided the source is acknowledged

The views expressed do not necessarily reflect those of Cedefop or the Commission

Printed in Belgium

Contents

Page

1. Foreword by Mr. Ivor Richard, Member of the European Commission, responsible for Employment, Social Affairs and Education ... 9

2. Technical note ... 13

3. Speeches made during the opening session of the seminar

    3.1 Mr Hywel Jones, Head of Division for Education and Training, Commission of the European Communities ... 19
    3.2 Mr Roger Faist, Director of CEDEFOP ... 31
    3.3 Ms Shirley Williams, Research Fellow, Policy Studies Institute, London ... 37
    3.4 Professor Henri Janne, Institute of Sociology, Free University of Brussels ... 55

4. New perspectives in continuing education and training in an enlarged European Community - a general working paper drawn up by the Education Services of the European Commission ... 65

5. Closing speech by Mr Jacques Delors, Director of the Research Centre "Work and society", University of Paris IX Dauphine ... 97

6. Conclusions and recommendations of the three working groups established during the seminar ... 121

Annexes

A   Seminar programme ... 163
B   List of participants ... 169
C   List of papers prepared on specific aspects of the three seminar themes ... 179

1. Foreword by Mr Ivor Richard

Member of the European Commission,
responsible for Employment, Social Affairs and Education

FOREWORD

Continuing education and training can make an essential contribution to social and economic development. Certain specialists working in the field may have long been aware of this fact. It is only very recently, however, as the European Community has plunged deeper into economic recession, that a wider political debate has begun to emerge on the need to establish a new relationship between work, education and leisure in adult life. Our societies are under increasing pressure to produce new capacities of innovations and flexibility and at the same time to prevent a widening of social and economic inequalities. It is against this background that the role of continuing education and training may be seen in a new light.

This report, summarizing the proceedings of the seminar which took place in Berlin in October 1980 will, I hope, serve to stimulate ideas for a new policy approach to continuing education and training. In organizing this seminar, the European Commission and the European Centre for the Development of Vocational Training (CEDEFOP) were especially concerned to bridge the gap which has traditionally separated the rather idealistic work of adult education and the more practical field of industrial training.

The seminar was a landmark in this respect. It brought together specialists from widely differing milieus including grass-roots practitioners and personalities such as Jacques Delors, Henri Janne, Bertrand Schwartz and Shirley Williams. What emerges from the report is an eloquent argument for a more integrated strategy for education and training. The report demonstrates some of the practical implications of such a strategy and touches on policy issues as diverse as job creation, illiteracy, early retirement, local community development, educational leave and work-sharing.

Many of the ideas developed at the seminar have since found further more concrete expression within Member States and at Community level. The European Commission has itself brought together within one portfolio responsibilities for education, training, employment and social affairs. A new spirit of inter-ministerial cooperation is emerging at the various Council meetings of Ministers of Finance, Employment and Education. In policy terms, the impact of the seminar at Community level has also been considerable.

I hope that this report will now enable a much wider audience to be associated with the ideas developed at the seminar and to take part in the gradual renewal of continuing education and training that is beginning to take place within the European Community.

Ivor Richard
Member of the Commission
of the European Communities

2. Technical note

TECHNICAL NOTE

1. The objective of the seminar was to provide an opportunity for a limited number of specialists from a wide range of backgrounds to take part in a joint reflection on the new challenges and opportunities facing continuing education and training in an enlarged Community.

2. The seminar programme can be found in Annex A of this report. A list of participants is contained in Annex B.

3. It will be seen that most of the work in the seminar took place in working groups, which concentrated on three distinct, but inter-related themes:

    (1) the development of basic adult education and literacy,

    (2) the role of continuing education and training as a preparation for new forms of employment and development,

    (3) the problems of older workers and the transition to retirement, and their implications for continuing education and training.

4. For the discussions the participants were able to draw on the general working paper, prepared by the services of the European Commission, as well as on the introductory speeches, the texts of which are included in this report.

Also available were reports on various aspects of the three themes prepared by experts for the seminar. These reports, which are listed in Annex C are available in all Community languages except for Greek, and may be obtained on request from either the Commission of the European Communities (Directorate-General for Employment, Social Affairs and Education) or from the European Centre for the Development of Vocational Training (CEDEFOP).

5. This report also includes the conclusions and recommendations resulting from the discussions of the three working groups and the text of a concluding speech.

3. Speeches made during the opening session of the seminar

3.1.
Mr Hywel Jones

Head of Division for Education and Training,
Commission of the European Communities

Mr Jones has, since the seminar, become Director for Education, Training and Youth Policy in the Directorate-General for Employment, Social Affairs and Education of the Commission

I should like to open this seminar and welcome you all to
Berlin on behalf of my Director General, Mr Günther Schuster,
for whom I am deputizing.
Critical budget discussions at the European Parliament in
Strasbourg, taking place today and tomorrow, prevented Mr Schuster,
to his very great regret, from being with us in Berlin today.
The shadow of budget discussions, taking place at all levels in
the Community, is indeed likely to hang over our discussion here
this week. We cannot and should not avoid this shadow if we are
to come to grips with the challenge posed by the theme of this
seminar. I shall have more to say about this in a moment. First,
however, I should like to thank you all for being here and to
say a few introductory words about the purpose of this seminar.

This is a seminar with a very particular and rather ambitious
objective. The Commission and the European Centre for the Development of Vocational Training, briefly but affectionately known
as CEDEFOP, have invited you to take part here in a "brainstorming" to assist the Commission at a critical stage in the preparation of ideas for a series of new initiatives in the areas
of continuing education and training.

We are pleased to welcome you here in your personal capacity,
not as delegates of individual Member States or of particular
organizations, but as individuals deeply committed in your fields
of work, therefore approaching the seminar theme from different
perspectives, but free to let your minds roam beyond your immediate professional concerns. We have sought particularly to
bring together here a wide diversity of professional experience
from adult education through to industrial training; from the
trade unions, employers, the voluntary organizations and from
academic and educational circles: from high positions with responsibility for policy formulation and from the grass roots
of practical experience. This diversity was the result of a
deliberate initiative, since the "social partners" are so often
absent from discussions on "education", whereas "training"

is often debated without the participation of educationalists. The very diversity among the participants here thus presents an important challenge: it underlines our conviction that the development of continuing education and training in the 1980s can only take off if we all in our different ways build bridges between the different actors and agencies in the field, establishing a common language of action and jointly identifying priorities for the future.

The general theme we are discussing is not new. The factors, which make it imperative to move towards a more coherent strategy for continuing education and training, are no longer really in dispute. Fresh points of gravity are emerging as a result of the introduction of the new information technologies. Each of us knows that we are ill-equipped to face up to the possibly immense consequences that microelectronics may have on our daily lives.

For most of us, however, it is the economic factors which are at the forefront of our preoccupations. Continuing unemployment at unprecedented levels throughout the Community is the symptom of a fundamental dislocation of our society and the consolidation of two groups in society: the "haves" and the "have nots". The consequent demands on the education and training systems, although still ill-defined, have radically changed since the period of economic growth experienced in most countries in the 1960s, and since the period in the early 70s when high rates of unemployed were still seen by many to be a passing phenomena.

It is in this context that nearly every Member State is engaged in making severe cuts in public expenditure which are having a profound effect on continuing education and training. It would be quite unrealistic for us here to ignore this reality or simply to hope for a substantial increase in public funding for continuing education and training in the near future.

This is not to be defeatist. Although budget cuts in certain areas of activity have already been so severe that long-established provisions are now being radically reduced, we must consider to what extent this creates an opportunity for a fundamental review of priorities and a reassessment of existing structures and of provision in the education and training field. There could emerge a positive side in this process in so far as it leads to a more integrated strategy on the use of resources and more sensitivity to local needs.

The further enlargement of the European Community presents an additional challenge to be taken into account in considering the scope for new initiatives at the Community level. Enlargement, to include Greece, Spain and Portugal, will - we hope - oblige the Community to reconsider economic and social policy together in the context of development policy. This may not be an easy process. As the Community expands and grows richer in its diversity, we must question more seriously how best to use Community instruments, particularly in an area where initiatives at local level, in response to local needs, have demonstrated a rare vitality and given a lead for future strategy. Although such initiatives may have been of peripheral interest at Community and at national level for some while, the time is now ripe to consider how to move the periphery to the centre of attention on the European stage.

THE CHALLENGES

The significance of local "community development" is underlined in the general working paper for this seminar. It reflects our concern to take continuing education and training back to the people, to be less concerned with "providing" and more concerned with "enabling" - enabling groups of people to make their own choices, develop their own activities and find new solutions together. The educational resources both formal and informal, which exist within local communities, are often still largely untapped but may well have a profound importance in the period of austerity facing us.

Recent initiatives to bring together local resources in
new combinations have been taken in connection with programmes
destined for young people, most particularly for the young unemployed. We have chosen to dwell on this phenomenon in the
working paper because so much of what is being developed for
young people, throughout the Community, is of equal if not
greater relevance to other generations. A major strategic question for
the seminar will be to consider how to reduce the traditional
preoccupation with age, amongst education and training and
employment circles. The current fashion for "alternance" and
the problems of "transition" from education to working life,
are still associated in most minds with policies for young
people under 20, yet there is an obvious and increasing need
to enable a much wider range of people to benefit from a more
balanced link between "work" and "non-work" time.

The starting points for reflection and discussion within
the working groups at this seminar have, I should explain,
been taken to illustrate a number of underlying preoccupations
of this sort. There is a general concern, clearly, for greater
equality of opportunity for all to lead a useful role in society.
This leads, in one direction, to a consideration of a more equitable distribution of opportunities for continuing education and
training. It leads, also, in another direction, to a review of
the role of continuing education and training in facilitating
the creation of useful activities by citizens, of whatever age,
in society. In both ways, the exploitation and reallocation of
available educational resources, in existing institutions,
through the media and so forth, must be considered.

Of course there are other priorities. We have not specifically
mentioned the implications of the trend towards industrial democracy, or the needs of specific categories such as migrant
workers plus their families or married women seeking to return
to the labour market. Nor have we discussed in detail the impact
and potential of microelectronics, and the growing need for the

adult population to master such new technologies. Some of these issues are the subject of specific programmes of activity at Community level which I will not dwell on here. Other issues such as the question of the training of adult educators or the problem of certification are, in our view, an essential part of wider problems which can be examined within the working groups.

THE COMMUNITY DIMENSION

I should emphasize that the three selected starting points for reflection are of particular relevance to policy development and policy instruments at Community level. Brief references to these are made in the working paper. You will not necessarily be very familiar with the various Community instruments in the area of continuing education and training or in related fields. One can say that there has in the past been a predominant emphasis on the functional labour market aspects of continuing education and training. And the Commission is endowed with elaborate instruments making significant financial intervention in this area. However, adult education in the traditional sense of the word has not been an area of major concern at Community level until now. This situation perhaps mirrors that at national level. It is also an indication of the rather narrow interpretation still given in some quarters to the founding treaties of the European Community relegating the wider social, cultural and humanitarian objectives of the European Community to a back seat position and thus preventing the development of any coherent inter-sectoral approach so far as continuing education and training is concerned. This situation is changing slowly.

In the educational field, several extensive programmes of cooperation have been developed since 1976, although Community competence even to cooperate in the field of education is still a subject of dispute. The net result of this situation is that, as at national level, debate within the educational sector tends to be isolated from action carried out in other policy sectors.

My department has already undertaken some preliminary work in the field of adult and continuing education in the last few years - we were for instance privileged to benefit from the collaboration of Prof. Henri Janne and Prof. Bertrand Schwartz for the preparation of a major report in this area, which drew together for our benefit the fruits of work done in other international and national structures. I am particularly happy to have both these distinguished experts with us here for this seminar.

The time has now come, we believe, to move the debate about the role of continuing education and training to the centre of the stage at the Community level, and consider its implications for the development of other Community policies, not just in the manpower field, but also as regards industrial, agricultural and regional policy. To this extent, the challenge we face at Community level is not unlike that posed at national level.

We are posing similar questions about the directions of social and economic policy as a whole, in order to identify the place of continuing education and training in the future.

For instance, we must challenge the wisdom of putting so much emphasis on job-related vocational training for the unemployed or for first entrants to the labour market. Focusing on the training needs of industry, when industry is patently unable to provide enough jobs for those in search of employment,

means in effect excluding from consideration large and
increasing numbers of people who find themselves on the
fringe of the primary labour market.

We must also, in this context, begin to question the forms
of consultation and decision making about social and employment policy. We are concerned that, particularly in the debate
on work sharing, the interests of those on the fringe of the
primary labour market, in self-employment, in casual employment, or those on the dole, do not come across as forcefully
as we should expect. Another example is our questioning of
the concept of regional policy which has tended to be dominated
by a concern to achieve a transfer of resources between regions
and by strategies to tempt external industrial investment to
those regions, honoured or stigmatized by the title of "under-
developed". It is this approach perhaps which has led to a
situation where the capacity for renewal and development within
and by local communities has been largely ignored.

As a further example, there are the policy measures destined
for specific industrial sectors, which tend to be inspired
by a narrow concern for preservation of an efficient industrial
base and to off-load the resulting social problem, caused
for instance by mass redundancies and premature retirement
schemes, into other agencies. All these areas of policy have
profound implications for continuing education and training.

We have dwelt at some length in the working paper on the need
to bridge the divide between education and training. This is
an only too familiar appeal. Much lip-service is currently
paid to this objective. I should stress that our aim here
goes much further. It is to build bridges between a whole
range of policy sectors in order to arrive at a more realistic
and more forward looking approach to the problem of social and
economic development.

This does not therefore necessarily lead us to the conclusion that more and more funds should be made available or that new directives and legislation are the right policy instruments to use in these circumstances. First and foremost we must use existing instruments: at Community level for example, we shall be looking very seriously with our colleagues in other sectors at the scope for the possible reorientation and further interaction between certain instruments such as the Social Fund, the Regional Fund and the guidance section of the Agricultural Fund (EAGGF). There must be a new commitment on the part of those involved in education and training to consider strategy very carefully. There have frankly been enough words and theories expended on the need for coherent strategies for continuing education and training without having made much impact on the reality, without having penetrated the thinking of those who influence policy making in other sectors.

I believe there is a most important role to be played in this direction by the exchange of experience and information about existing examples of action directed towards local community development. Not just examples of pilot schemes which tend to benefit from additional financial resources and benevolent flexibility by authorities. No, we should be particularly interested in demonstrating how action can be taken within the existing frameworks, showing how schools, manpower authorities, voluntary organizations, and local councillors can work together at local level, irrespective of the apparent constraints on coordination at national level.

I believe in the power of example, and I consider this is an area where the Community can make a vital contribution by spreading ideas and perhaps making certain ideas more respectable across a broad political spectrum and thus modifying the terms of the general debate by making the general public and politicians aware of needs and possibilities; by making available to those seeking change at grass roots level examples which can be exploited for their purposes.

So, in conclusion, this seminar will be looking at how to build a strategy and how to develop a common language of action. I hope, in the working groups, you will be able to identify particular areas where the European Community could play an important promotional role. My colleagues here will be listening very carefully to what you all have to say and after the seminar, we shall set to with the drafting of a consultative document -a "green paper"- which we hope to circulate for comments during the early part of the New Year. By this time next year, we hope to be in a position to propose to the Council of Ministers of the European Community the outline of an action programme for the 1980s.

I wish you well in your discussions -which should be frank and outspoken. I hope that your experience will be rich and rewarding for each of you personally and that you will continue to be associated with our endeavours in this field.

I would thank the European Centre here in Berlin very warmly for offering to host this seminar and for working so closely with us in its preparation. I hope that participants here at the seminar will make use of this opportunity to acquaint themselves further with various activities and publications of CEDEFOP in different areas of vocational training.

3.2. Mr Roger Faist
Director of Cedefop

3.2.
Mr Roger Faist
Director of Cedefop

WELCOMING SPEECH

by Mr Roger Faist
Director of CEDEFOP

In my turn I would also like to welcome you.

Situated, as we are on the borders of Europe, we are always happy to be able to welcome to Berlin those with whom we work, who are active in the field of vocational training, and to give them an opportunity to compare directly their experiences. This meeting is different and its objective is more important than a simple comparison of experiences. What we and DG XII wish to do is to provide an opportunity for reflection and at the same time for consultation, with leading European experts, on a Community plan for development of continuing education and training.

In this way CEDEFOP responds to its double objective of providing a forum for ideas and of helping the Commission in its work.

Your conclusions and the comments you make on the proposals which you receive will make it possible to advance towards recognition of the role of continuing education and training in Community policy-making.

It is curious to note that education is not mentioned
in the Treaty of Rome, although vocational training
is explicitly indicated as an area of Community action.

Without reviewing the progress of education and training
in the history of the European institutions, let us say
that this sharp dichotomy has not been conducive to a global approach, particularly, to the development of a European policy for the education and training of adults.

In the absence of a precise framework, CEDEFOP has
up until now conducted two activities.

The first one has been concerned with researching
innovations in the field of the education and training
of adults, where the experiences are as varied, as the
systems are badly defined. We have therefore created a
network, identified 1 500 bodies concerned with continuing education and training, and published a collection
of innovatory actions in continuing education and training.

The second has, so to speak, consisted of an alternative
approach to that of training/employment, by trying to
substitute for it a training/development approach. On the
basis of experiences noted in Italy, France and the United
Kingdom, we have been able to identify some new models
of education and training which are more spontaneous, more
oriented towards the creation, rather than the saving,
of jobs, and in every case more motivating for individuals
and the communities concerned.

We can, and will go further. We will, however, be more effective if this seminar allows the Commission to draw up elements for guidelines for more general action for the years to come.

Without trying to cover again all the ideas proposed for your consideration, I would like to make my contribution by suggesting four points to you.

What purpose can education and training have for people for whom work has no purpose or, for people to whom work does not permit any initiative and gives no chance to discover and exploit their abilities? Every consideration of training for tomorrow should take into account the content of work available and the risks of polarization between qualified and unqualified work.

To reduce alternance (linked work and training) to the last phase of initial education and to the period of transition from school to work, would be an error. Surely the whole problem of continuing education and training is in effect a problem of alternance?

I am always struck by how little linkage is made between the experiences of continuing education and training and those of initial education and training. Are the initial education systems so impervious to change? To consider continuing education and training for tomorrow is also to raise questions about the capacity of the educational systems to adapt themselves in order to be open to the idea of lifelong education and training.

Lastly, to think of continuing education and training tomorrow is also to take into account the new challenges which recent technological evolution poses, particularly in the field of mini- and micro-data processing and the distance processing of information. It is important not to use all the forces of education and training too late. It is important, faced with this new challenge, to surmount the religious wars between educators and trainers. Our livelihoods, not just our present jobs, are at stake, and not only ours, but also those of our children.

I am sure that you have already had ideas such as these. It is now up to you to make your proposals and for us to listen to you.

3.3. Ms Shirley Williams

Research Fellow, Policy Studies Institute, London
Ms Williams was Secretary of State for Education and Science
in the United Kingdom from 1976 to 1979

It is difficult to decide what education policy should be at a time of such massive change as the industrialized world is passing through at the present time. It is almost impossible to project the society in which our children are going to live when they reach the prime of their lives. In earlier centuries, and indeed still in many more traditional parts of the world, children learnt from their parents and grandparents the thing that they needed to know. They learnt about the patterns of the seasons, the behaviour of animals, the nature of the soil, how to carve wood, and how to build houses. The traditional wisdom of their elders retained unbroken the pattern of authority passed down from generation to generation. But today that authority is broken by the speed of change itself; children may know more about the most modern things like space travel, or even microelectronics, than their teachers do, let alone their parents. This is part of the crisis of authority which creates such difficulties for the structure of education. It is also one reason why the authority, both moral and intellectual, of a child's peer group seems so much greater than it did a couple of generations ago.

The changes are not only technological ones, they are also related to the massive alteration in the pattern of resources available for the future, a pattern so different than it was in the 1950s or 1960s that it raises a very large question mark about the whole prospect for economic growth. Oil prices have risen 16-fold since 1973, and perhaps at least as significant the price of oil is now set by the oil producers of the Middle East rather than the Texas Railroad Commission. The prices of other sources of energy, such as coal and natural gas, are rising alongside the price of oil and clearly the days of cheap energy are now over. The repercussions of this on other raw materials are very substantial as well. Therefore, the collapse in growth projections with the

OECD's own figures having fallen from the $2^1/2$ %
per annum growth rate in 1980 projected in January 1979
for the Western nations to less than half of 1 %
at the present time, may not only reflect the impact of
the world recession but a much more profound structural
change underlying the whole of the economic prospects of
the industrialized world. Clearly we face the prospect
of massively high unemployment rates, especially among
the young, with the ratio of unemployed under the age of
24 being of the order of twice the adult rate, or even
three times the adult rate, in many OECD countries.
The projections for next year already indicate figures
of between 13 and 16 %   unemployment among young
people in Canada Britain, France, the United States,
Denmark and other countries besides. For tragically
the slow down in world growth and the possibly more
fundamental break in the whole pattern of dependence
on cheap energy and raw materials on the part of the
industrialized nations has coincided with the highest
age groups reaching the labour market for very many
decades past. Not only have there been record numbers
of 16 year olds coming forward for work in the last two
years, figures that will go on remaining very high until
the middle of the 1980s, but the high youth age groups
coincide with a low retirement rate among the relatively
small number of old people who started work 45 and 50
years ago, just after the end of the First World War.
There is still a considerable rise in the rate of employment activity among married women who are often now in
our countries found to be competing with young people
for the jobs available.

Nor is this the end of the litany of matters with which
we should be concerned and about which we should be
profoundly disturbed. On top of the wave of recession and the
wave of young people entering the labour market we have

the growing impact of the new technologies. There
are many new technologies, not only one, ranging from
the arrival of the microprocessor to the first intimations
of biotechnology, which may open up a whole new world
of resources created by the manipulation and cloning of
general material. The one, however, that for the purposes
of this lecture I am particularly concerned about is
microelectronics, which promises the possibility of
automated offices, computer controlled machines, flexible
robots and computer-assisted design by the end of this
decade, if not earlier. Studies done both in West Germany
and internationally indicate the likelihood of a reduction
in office jobs of between 30 and 40 % rising as
high as 60 or 70 % in the case of government and
local government administration. Further studies indicate
that there could also be very substantial losses in
such fields as technical drawing and draughtsmanship,
extending also to areas of the professions such as
banking and insurance, particularly in the middle management grades. In my own country the electronic exchange
has vastly reduced the number of men and women employed
in producing the necessary hardware but also in the
numbers engaged in the actual operation of the exchanges
as compared with the electro-mechanical exchanges that
preceded them. Finally, there is the growing competition
from the newly-industrialized nations of the Third World,
both for resources and for markets. It is quite clear
that the West has no future ahead of it trying to compete
with these highly efficient countries with their substantially lower unit costs of labour in the field of
electrical and electronic goods. The West to survive
will have to move up market. In this intensive competition
for markets with the newly-industrialized countries of
the Third World the older industrialized countries will
have to move on to more sophisticated processes and products
if they are to survive. They are often said to

have one great advantage, their education systems. Most
have had compulsory primary education for a century!
many have had compulsory secondary education for a
generation or more. Almost all the citizens of the OECD
countries and of the Soviet bloc are literate, most are
basically numerate, and a large minority have more
advanced professional and technical qualifications.

This educational foundation gives the older industrial
countries a head start in exploiting the new technologies,
which require basic understanding of language and mathematics, and some knowledge of how to handle and organize
information. It is the greatest advantage they have, since
their costs of labour are much higher than in the newly
industrializing countries. Switzerland and Sweden have
shown that countries with few natural advantages can
sustain high standards of living by the intelligent
deployment of a highly qualified workforce. But the
key phrase is "highly qualified". The older industrial
countries cannot risk a decline in the quality of their
education and training. Yet financial resources are under
great pressure, and expenditure on education is unlikely
to grow at a time when pupil numbers are falling fast.

It is necessary to stand back a little and ask what kind
of education the majority of people will need in the
modern industrial world, or even in the post-industrial
world, the information society. No one can say for sure.
But where technological change is rapid, a broad foundation
on which different skills can be built offers the soundest
answer. Men and women will have to understand the new
technologies well enough to be able to participate in
sensible decisions about how they are used and for what ends.

So the citizens of our democracies will need at least
a nodding acquaintance with computers, microprocessors
and technology more generally. They should be able to
use mathematics as they can use language, that is be
basically numerate as well as basically literate. And
they will need to know at least a little about economics
and the society of which they are part, nationally and
internationally, to contribute to new structures of
industrial democracy and local community initiatives.

Boys and girls also need to be prepared for these social
changes in modern society. Even if long periods of unemployment can be avoided, hours of work are likely to
be shorter, and holidays longer. People will need to
be educated to use their leisure time enjoyably, to be
able to exploit the opportunities open to them according
to their individual choice. The emergence of women as
equal citizens (though high unemployment could seriously
prejudice its evolution) implies a fairer distribution
of domestic and family responsibilities between men and
women. This has clear consequences for the curriculum,
some of them already being recognized in the way subjects
like domestic science and woodwork are now being taught
to both boys and girls.

In any educational structure dominated by public examinations as that of Britain is (and as most of the structures in Western Europe are), the curriculum can only be
reformed if the examinations are reformed too. So a
broadly based secondary curriculum, in which most subjects
have to be taken by all children up to the age of 16,
will require that the examinations themselves offer fewer
options, or, in other words, that the examinations cease
to require such early choices of the subjects in which
the children will specialize.

Even a broadening of the curriculum will only influence tangentially the most acute division of all in education, the split between academic and vocational education. Vocational education everywhere in Europe has long been the form of further education reserved for the socially inferior. Bright working-class boys get apprenticeships. Bright middle-class boys - and girls too - go to university. The massive expansion of higher education in the last 20 years has enabled far more bright working-class boys and girls to go on to higher education. But they are still only a small fraction of the total, at most one in four (Britain, as it happens, has the highest proportion of working-class youngsters in higher education of any Western European country, but that proportion has not changed in 20 years). Few middle-class young people take apprenticeships, though graduate unemployment has persuaded some to do so in Denmark and West Germany, sometimes after graduation. Generally speaking, the two tracks remain separate and there is little intermeshing between them. Yet the divorce between the thinkers and the makers, those that study and those that do, is one of the most profound sources of social difference, and influences society's attitudes towards manufacturing industry as against the professions. Victorian England's distaste for those in trade as distinct from gentlemen and scholars is embedded deep in the educational system, and not only in England.

It is this segregation that Sweden and Denmark are now tackling in their upper secondary schools, trying to bring together vocational courses and academic courses, and allowing young people to put together combinations of both. It is not only geographical integration that is

needed, however. High attainment in vocational courses
should be recognized as a qualification for entry to higher
education just as A levels are. The Government of France
decided in 1976 to recognize technological qualifications -
roughly the French equivalent of HND -not only for entry
to higher education, but also to the prestigious grandes
écoles, including the Ecole Nationale d'Administration,
which leads to the highest posts in the French civil service.
Despite this revolutionary step, French upper secondary
education is still divided between academically oriented
schools and technically oriented schools; the Scandinavians
have gone much further.

Vocational education in Britain, as in France, is largely
segregated into separate institutions, the colleges of
further education, while the school sixth forms concentrate
on academic studies. But there has been a gradual coming
together. Further education colleges offer O level and A
level courses to their students in a wide range of subjects.
Sixth forms have begun to add technical courses and business
courses for the "non-academic sixth", youngsters who stay
on for a year or even two to get professional qualifications.
The Business Education Council and the Technical Education
Council have candidates for their examinations both from
the schools and from the colleges.

The most highly integrated combination of academic and
vocational education is found in the tertiary colleges,
which take in all the 16 year-olds in a particular
area, whether they intend to take vocational subjects,
academic subjects, or a combination of both, and whether
they are full-time or part-time. The opportunities for
students to mix socially and in extra-curricular activities
make traditional distinctions between vocational and academic seem absurd; each group learns something about the

work of the other. Given the extreme pressures on
financial resources, a national network of tertiary
colleges is unlikely to be achieved for many years
to come; however, other areas have sixth form colleges
or community schools, which can help to bridge the
divide between vocational and academic education. The
sixth form college can offer a combined range of courses
alongside the further education college, allowing students to take some courses in one institution and some
in the other. Sixth forms in schools can do the same,
though their much more limited size makes timetabling
difficult. The sixth form college can also open its
doors to adult students who would like to study a particular subject, since most student groups are small
and teachers can easily manage a few additional students.
Segregation of age-groups is as well-established in
education as the academic/vocational divide. But community schools, one of the most exciting recent developments in British education, already do include adult
students in many of their classes, though some limit
their participation to classes outside school hours,
or to classes in subjects such as art, metalwork and
pottery. The community school means what its name says;
its facilities are shared with the local neighbourhood,
it is open from early in the morning until late at night,
and it is part of the community rather than separated from
it, as so many traditional secondary schools still are.
In purpose-built community schools, gymnasiums, playing
fields, assembly halls, theatres, craft and common rooms
are open to adults in the local community, just as they
are to children. Old people's clubs and mother and
baby clubs meet within the school premises. Education

becomes visibly not just the occupation of youth, but part of lifelong experience. Many of the traditional secondary schools are embracing new commitments to the community too. As pupil numbers fall, and they will fall by a third in the secondary schools in the present decade, empty classrooms are being used for nursery groups or for classes for the young unemployed. Declining numbers make life very difficult for schools, especially if financial resources are cut correspondingly; but they do offer opportunities too, as they provide spare space and buildings, which can be used with imagination. For instance, many adults need a second chance of education; in Britain 50 000 people volunteered to teach illiterate adults, and 100 000 became literate. Many hundreds more have taught English to non-English speaking immigrants.

One problem in bringing vocational education and academic education closer together is the separate salary scales, different working conditions and sometimes different qualifications required of teachers. Everywhere in Western Europe these differences have made greater integration difficult. In Britain, the Burnham negotiations for school teachers are conducted separately from those for college teachers, and salary structures are quite distinct. Bringing salary structures, regulations and requirements together is a tedious job, but it is essential if the two strands of education, academic and vocational are at last to be integrated.

The repercussions of integration between academic and vocational education involve higher education also. The division between the universities and the polytechnics, the "binary system", was established in Britain in 1967 by Antony Crosland, then the Secretary of State for Education and Science, in order to encourage the polytechnics to be very different institutions from the universities. He wanted them to attract mature students part-time students and students studying for qualifications other than degrees, and he hoped that they would identify with their local communities, since they would be financed largely from local government sources and not by the University Grants Commission. But the polytechnics, like their predecessors, the colleges of advanced technology, have been attracted by the university model. While they retain some differences, particularly a greater emphasis on technology, their student bodies resemble those of the universities in having a preponderance of young men and women, studying full-time for a first degree. As the numbers of these undergraduate students fall, through the late 1980s, both the universities and the polytechnics will have an opportunity to widen their intake. The polytechnics, unlike the universities, have catered for part-time students to some extent, but there is plenty of scope for attracting more mature students, students on in-service and refresher courses, and those studying at home for short residential periods. The institutions of higher education in Britain, as in most of Western Europe, do not see themselves as resource centres for their own cities or counties in the way American universities do. But there need be no tension between this role and the role of being an internationally recognized centre of academic excellence. The University of California, for instance, manages both roles without damaging its reputation.

The reforms proposed in the public examination system would entail a less specialized first degree course, as universities are quick to point out. The more specialized courses

would then have to be taken at postgraduate level, as
they are in the United States, and there would have to
be more "taught" postgraduate courses which might be no
bad thing. In fact, broader first degree courses would
fit into the requirements of the new society. Many of
the new developments require several disciplines to be
brought together. Biotechnology, for instance, involves
biologists, chemists, chemical engineers, biochemists,
molecular biologists and electronic engineers in working
together. Because of the high degree of specialization
in science, such cooperation is not easy. Microeclectronics
will, as we have seen, affect a huge range of activities
from schoolteaching to engineering maintenance. The men
and women educated in a narrow speciality will find it
difficult to adapt to the change. As for the civil service
into which so many of the more able graduates go, would it
not benefit from the entry of young men and women with at
least a rudimentary knowledge of science and technology
as well as of philosophy, history and politics?

Let me turn back for the last part of what I want to say
from higher education to those of our people most at risk,
the children who have suffered from disadvantages either
because they are the children of the inner city coming
from a deprived and often bitter environment or because
their parents belong to ethnic minorities, often in poor
and unskilled jobs. Many of these latter also face the
barrier of language and almost all of them face the barrier
of prejudice of the host community. In some countries
prejudice arises simply by the chance of sex, because they
are girls rather than boys. I spent much of the last year
looking at youth unemployment in the different countries
of the EEC and OECD and again and again I was struck by
the fact that even the appalling general level of unemployment among young people in most of our countries becomes

markedly higher in the case of these deprived children. It is quite simply scandalous that we do readily accept the unemployment of the educationally disadvantaged, of children from the ethnic minorities and of working-class girls, for whom employment often gives meaning to their lives since they are so much less well-equipped to enjoy leisure activities or to travel than the more fortunate children of the middle and professional classes. The central question is what can be done for these children.

The answer is to be found in many areas but not least in the transition from school to work. The transition can be assisted at the most simple level by courses to familiarize young people with the world of work, with such obvious things as the necessity to appear on time, to wear the right sort of clothes, to write the right sort of letters in order to get an interview for a job, and to simply understand what the working world is all about. Even the very basic simple training offered, for example under the British Youth Opportunities Programme which has work experience courses lasting for six months and sometimes less, can be a Godsend to a young person. It is interesting that under the Youth Opportunities Programme, which in 1979 offered some kind of training or work experience opportunity to more than 200 000 young people, all but a few hundred of the young unemployed who applied, the rate of placement among the young people who passed through these courses was remarkably high. After three months more than 80 % of them were employed and of that more than 80 % half were employed by the employers who had taken them on in the first place. The truth of the matter is that familiarization is not only for young people but is also for employers, many of

whom are acutely suspicious of a young generation they
do not communicate easily with and know very little about.

At the other end of the spectrum there is a much more
elaborate apprenticeship system in West Germany, Austria
and Switzerland, under which some 90 % of school
leavers get an apppprenticeship involving not only training
on the job but also a day or more than a day a week of
theoretical training in educational colleges or group
training centres. I have my criticisms of the Austro-
German system. I believe it starts too early and is
too rigid in slotting children into the spaces pre-
ordained for them, without sufficient consideration of
the child's own wishes or own potential. Nevertheless
it has to be said that there are few systems which more
effectively assist the disadvantaged youngster to find
some sort of niche in the world. The system is not so
effective when it comes to those who are highly disadvantaged such as girls from working-class homes or
children of immigrant families; West Germany needs to
do a great deal of work in these fields, but one has to
say that it is an impressive system and one from which
the rest of us have much to learn. I believe one of the
things that we can learn from it is the necessity to write
off against tax the cost of training so as to provide a
real incentive to industry to make a major contribution
to the up-grading and up-skilling of young people.
But even all this is not enough. In the information society
towards which we are moving it will simply be inadequate
to provide an initial training for young people. The very
fact of change means that many skills learned through
an apprenticeship will turn out to be inappropriate or
obsolete in a world that we can hardly begin to plot the
path of. Furthermore, my own belief is that there will

be more and more emphasis on the conserving aspects
of society and on the community aspects so that many
young people who start life, for example, in manufacturing may well end their lives working in a self-sufficient
community or on such things as solar energy or the intensive
raising of vegetables or fish. This means that, even more
than at present, people will have to go back to be retrained or reeducated. So my concept is that every young person
in addition to getting some kind of structured transition
from school to work, including training of various lengths
leading to skill or professional qualifications, will in
addition take with him a commitment by Federal or local
or central government to his right to be trained later
in life, perhaps for three or four years in all, to be
taken at any time that he wishes. Such a commitment, in
a sense a kind of pledge by the community to a person's
continuing education, could be taken up by that person
either in the form of a formal retraining course or it
could be taken in the form of the widening of his own
personal education, including education for leisure or
for retirement, or it could be taken as a series of refresher courses, for example for teachers or doctors,
during the course of their working career. Basically the
concept is that the idea that many of our countries
have adopted, that is to say that any young person who
qualifies to enter higher education will in fact receive
the financial support necessary to get through, would
be extended to the whole of life and to all groups in
the community in such a way that we would enter in to
a lifelong commitment to be taken as suits the individual,
but with obvious limits on what the financial commitment of
the community to it can be. I am not incidentally suggesting
that the whole amount needs to be publicly financed.

It could be, to use British parlance, means tested against the income of the individual concerned. Because this is one of the ways in which we can best help the disadvantaged or those who drop out of education because they are tired of school or perhaps have been badly taught, it is absolutely essential that there should be no financial barrier to people being able to return to education throughout their lives. It also has one further very crucial advantage as far as young women are concerned, that it enables them to return to take up their further education if necessary when their children have reached the age at which they can be left for periods of time so that the young woman can conduct her life in a way that suits her best. Nobody who understands the problems of living the dual life that most women have to live if they are mothers, or have other family responsibilities, will underestimate the barriers thrown up by the sheer formality of the education system and the extent to which it is still largely devoted to the education of those aged between 5 and 25.

There is much else that might be said about the future, not least because the repercussion of the new technology will hit everything from the pattern of social life, including the structure of cities, to the question of how far people will themselves be made obsolete by their coming. Above all what we have to recognize is that the new technologies must be made subordinate to people and not the other way round. The industrial society's greatest crime has been that it has so often moulded men and women to the needs of machinery. We have now reached the time when we can be emancipated. Have we got the wisdom to recognize that man is the measure of all things and that the time has come when that famous statement of the classical Greek philosopher should be realized in our society?

3.4. Professor Henri Janne

Président du Collège Scientifique, Institute of Sociology, Free University of Brussels
Professor Janne was Minister for Education and Culture
in Belgium between 1963 and 1965

PLENARY SESSION
OPENING ADDRESS [1]

Professor Henri Janne
Institute of Sociology
Free University of Brussels

Permit me at the outset to stress the need to remain within the framework outlined for the purposes of our four-day discussion, for the subject-matter does indeed furnish scope for the most widely strewn digressions.

(...)

Our seminar will keep to four parameters:
- the _future_ (the near future because the needs are urgent),
- the _continuing_ nature of education,
- the _European Community_,
- the definition of the subjects of the three working groups (adult basic education, new forms of work and development, and older workers).

I. Adult basic education and literacy

(After making reference to some of the proposals included in the working documents and stressing in particular that it would be erroneous to consider this problem complex to be a marginal issue, Professor Janne proceeded straight away to submit to the plenary assembly a number of proposals for examination.

In his capacity as general rapporteur of Project No 3 of the Council of Europe, he will take up these proposals again in Strasbourg on the occasion of the opening of the review conference on this project).

---

(1) This is a shortened version of Professor Janne's statement. The full text, in French, is available from CEDEFOP.

... "It is thus a global problem. The European Community should draw the following conclusions:

1. The Directorates General of the Commission should all work towards arriving at an integral policy which mobilizes all types of training resource; the Social Fund (efforts to prevent the marginalization of disadvantaged workers) and the Regional Fund (efforts aspiring to the same objective within geographically defined development areas) should adopt the same line of action.

2. In this context the EC should establish minimum criteria for basic education and the minimal conditions required for an adequate response to training needs (institutions, organization, content and methodology; creation of the necessary time resources, with the equally necessary financial compensation provisions; validation of training by means of appropriate certification, etc.).

3. One structural condition appears henceforth to represent an established principle: the need to integrate all educational resources at local level for purposes of basic training; in this way, the needs and the minimal response to satisfy these needs could lead to an adjustment of their general definition (at Community and/or Member State level) to suit the specific local conditions prevailing for the milieux in question.

4. The local integration of resources as a response to locally specified requirements implies a need for the decentralization of the major public and private establishments engaged in this field; these should in turn confer a large measure of autonomy and responsibility to the levels of application and practice.

5. The principles of local integration and global decentralization should not only be applied to education/training institutions and associations but also (by integrating all parties into one well-coordinated whole) to social services, firms, voluntary associations pursuing

social aims and to individual volunteers insofar as they all already assume or at least could usefully assume educational functions (in many instances by playing the role of mediator, a function which is preconditional for all further progress).

6. Two consequences can be drawn from this concept:
   - Services and associations whose primary objective is not educational should train, where necessary with assistance, their "mediators" to discharge the educational function incorporated in their activities; this raises several problems, including that of the educational status of the firm, which cannot simply acquire arbitrary control over its training rights and obligations; this problem is part of the overall problem complex concerning industrial democracy.
   - This approach to the basic training problem implies that educational activities should be made an integral part of a local community development plan."

(Professor Janne then proceeded to prove the feasibility of his recommendations by suggesting more efficient use of unemployment benefits, recourse to unemployed teaching personnel or to those in early retirement for purposes of servicing adult education measures, and a more intensive utilization of the media and modern educational techniques.)

II. Continuing training preparing for new forms of work and development

(Professor Janne underlined, as he later did in connection with the third discussion point, the interrelations between this and the other two discussion items.)

(He then proceeded to make a distinction between formal employment and other, non-institutionalized forms of employment. With reference to formal employment, he pointed out three categories "in which the need for new forms of work and development are socially localized": young people seeking their first job, women who have been made redundant or who cannot find access to working life, and older workers.)

(He then elaborated some reflections on "rigid" labour and also on "moonlighting" as a forerunner of more flexible forms of work which are "compatible with the needs and aspirations of certain marginalized parts of our society".)

These new forms of work, with reward and remuneration, are tending to become consolidated in line with norms displaying the following profile:

1. Part-time work (without prejudice to social security, annual leave and retirement conditions); in particular, part-time work should be admissible without incurring a total loss of unemployment benefit and without having proportionate repercussions on early pension or pension rights.

2. Temporary work, provided that this is controlled so that it can no longer degenerate into a form of exploitation (a cooperative form or work organization by official employment services appear to be acceptable solutions here).

3. A system of remunerated periods of in-firm work for young people (possibly with continued payment, at least partially, of the unemployment benefit, this now becoming a subsidy for the employer and thus an incentive to recruit young workers); if applied on a broad scale, this formula could permit the establishment of an institutionalized system of alternating work and study periods and would thus ensure a smooth transition between school and working life (the need for such a smooth transition is likewise evident between working life and retirement).

4. <u>Teamwork among young unemployed persons on a cooperative basis</u> as a response to a need for goods and services, of an ad hoc, permanent nature (maintenance, stocktaking, filing, accounting, transportation, specialized instruction, repairs, etc.).

5. <u>Personalized services</u>: some social services (in particular the health and education services) should be "personalized", i.e. should be tailored to suit the needs of the individual <u>without the individual having to be removed from his daily life sphere</u>...

   Basically, cumbersome organizations, in particular hospitals and schools, are nothing but a <u>poor and alienating substitute</u> for care provision within the individual's <u>own life sphere</u>. The "liberation" of a substantial workforce by the economic crisis could permit services to become personalized, with all the new work forms that such services would bring with them and the forms of training they would require.

6. <u>Multi-occupational status</u>: there are precedents for this concept - work in the mountain valleys, seasonal alternation between animal rearing and industrial work (in a nearby agglomeration or at home); there is also the example of the teacher-cum-parish-secretary-cum-local tourist guide, etc.

   Permit me to digress in order to examine some genuinely positive prospects in this connection: the structure of the <u>post-industrial society</u> could, in future, comprise two sectors, major organizations producing goods and services to satisfy standard, elementary needs (including basic agricultural products) on the one hand and an independent sector on the other for agricultural production, the crafts, personalized services, artistically and culturally creative activities (enterprises limited in size and organized on a cooperative basis which, in the event of successful operation, could split into a number of similar, smaller units). <u>Simultaneously and consecutively</u>, every man and woman would have two statuses and would pursue two activities in parallel:

- that of <u>manual worker, employee, technician or scientist</u> within a major production unit (according to qualifications, with continuing training opportunities being offered), this type of activity covering a period which would continually decrease in all respects (working day, working week, working year) with the spread of <u>electronics</u>;

- that of an independent worker in <u>a profession, a craft, in commerce or in an artistic or cultural field</u> (at all qualification levels) for an indefinite duration which would progressively increase.

The remuneration earned from the large-scale production sector should suffice to guarantee a decent minimum living standard, while the income gained from independent work should represent a supplementary income without limitation except in the form of a progressively structured taxation of income.

It is evident that this multiple-occupation status could represent the point of departure for a <u>policy of societal transformation</u> in line with technological progress (necessary with population densities such as they are) and current aspirations for more freedom and greater creativity. Security and liberty are thus, in principle, by no means incompatible.

By virtue of their very nature, the new forms of work would require <u>permanent and decentralized</u> opportunities for training. The trade unions in particular should adjust themselves to adopting a much more personalized approach to the negotiation and defence of these special forms of working condition. This entire "problematique" would generate training needs at all levels.

(Developing his thesis further, Professor Janne described the perspectives opened up by "activities which are novel with regard to their nature and which are non-profit-making from a market viewpoint". He notes in this connection that all such activities relate to a greater or lesser extent to "training-production" and thus require a complete deschooling of educational provision.)

III. Older workers, the transition towards retirement, and retirement

(Having outlined an "integrated" concept, Professor Janne examined this topic in the light of topics 1 and 2. He also pointed out an interesting characteristic of this target group—its non-homogeneity, a characteristic which again caused him to plead for flexibility of approach.)

"That which is required by this age group is a highly flexible status offering optimal protection, a smooth transition from working life to retirement (in the form most appropriate to the circumstances of each case), work opportunities (remunerated or voluntary) and satisfying occupations.

Such occupations could include:

- personalized services;

- assistance in educational provision;

- assistance in minding pre-school-age children (in the patriarchal family of the past, the grandparents used to educate children who had not yet reached the age at which they could assist their parents in their long daily work in the field or the workshop);

- occasional or auxiliary work as a prolongation of the former occupation;

- counselling and mediation contacts between disadvantaged persons and the public administrations and services;
- work to compensate the hours lost to an employer on account of young persons pursuing an alternating approach to work and study .

All this presupposes appropriate training opportunities for older persons and a decentralization of training modes and work organization."

(To conclude his address, Professor Janne emphasized the importance of the notion of guidance and reiterated the postulates of the concept of lifelong education.)

Original: French
Trans.: Ex LM

4. New perspectives in continuing education and training in an enlarged European Community

A general working paper drawn up by the Education Services of the European Commission

XII/936/80 - EN
rev.

NEW PERSPECTIVES IN CONTINUING EDUCATION AND TRAINING IN
AN ENLARGED EUROPEAN COMMUNITY

General Working Paper drawn up by Commission departments
(revised in September, 1981)

I. <u>The role of continuing education and training</u>

   1. A pragmatic definition
   2. Participation and development
   3. Adaptation and change

II. <u>Trends in continuing education and training</u>

   1. Words and deeds
   2. The education of adults - from individual demands to collective needs
   3. Continuing vocational training: from labour market demands to individual needs
   4. Young people: towards a synthesis
   5. Dynamism at the periphery
   6. The use of time

III. <u>Towards a more integrated strategy</u>

   1. A new scenario
   2. The distribution of time
   3. The concept of social and economic development

IV. <u>A role for the European Community</u>

   1. The prospects opened up by the second enlargement of the Community
   2. A number of starting points
   3. The potential of existing instruments
   4. Systems of interaction

I. THE ROLE OF CONTINUING EDUCATION AND TRAINING

1. A pragmatic definition

Continuing education and training consists, in its broadest sense of any form of learning activity, outside the content of the formal education system and of initial vocational training, designed to satisfy any individual or collective need or interest. It is not the task here to refine this definition. The concept of continuing education and training has been extensively developed in various guises, in the past two decades.[1] International organizations, such as UNESCO, the Council of Europe and the OECD have made an exceptional contribution in this direction.

If emphasis is given in some cases to provisions for 'adults', meaning those who are over the statutory school-leaving age or those who have left full-time education, attention still has to be given to reviewing the function of basic education and the structure of post-compulsory education, both in order to prepare young people for a pattern of life-long learning and in order to make full use of all available educational and training resources.

If in other cases a particular focus is placed on the "return" to formal studies, on a recurrent basis, full account must nevertheless be taken of the students' background and learning from real life experience.

---

(1) See, inter alia, "The development of permanent education in Europe" by Henri Janne and Bertrand Schwartz, Commission of the European Communities, Studies Collection, Education Series No 3.

2. Participation and development

Continuing education can play a particularly significant role in the context of strategies for social and economic development.

In a period of upheaval and uncertainty, such as is currently being experienced by West European societies at the beginning of the 1980s, when social and economic structures are undergoing profound changes, continuing education can assist individuals not only to understand and adapt to a changing environment but also to participate in the process of change.

In a situation where whole sections of the population are in danger of being progressively pushed to the fringes of society, there is, however, an increased need for continuing education to play a preventive as well as a remedial role, as part of a more comprehensive strategy aimed at preserving or promoting equal opportunities in society. Moreover, with the constant increase in remote forms of planning, decision-making and control, by bureaucracies, industrial conglomerates or whatever, there is an ever greater need to enable citizens, acting individually or collectively, to develop new forms of participation and control over their everyday lives.

3. Adaptation and change

The increasing complexity of modern society, dominated now by rapidly evolving technology, makes it more evident than in the past than an apprenticeship for adult life cannot be completed within one preliminary phase of schooling, isolated from practical personal experience of society. The efficient functioning of contemporary society demands that continuing education gradually becomes an integral part of the policies pursued in fields as diverse as industrial innovation, rural and regional development, energy conservation, immigration and social equality.

II. TRENDS IN CONTINUING EDUCATION AND TRAINING

1. Words and deeds

Many of the major developments in continuing education have reflected the misleading dichotomy between 'education' and 'training', between the 'non-functional' needs of the individual compared with the 'functional' needs of society, seen mainly in terms of the national labour market.

This dichotomy dates from a period when provisions for initial education were expected to provide an adequate aptitudinal basis for life in a stratified society, whereas vocational or job-specific skills were typically acquired at the work place or through specially-designed vocational training courses organized in various ways.

Even under the school systems existing today, within which in many countries 'vocational' education is an integral element, general education enjoys higher social prestige than vocational education. For those already outside the educational system, the dichotomy between education and vocational training is reinforced by the other traditional dichotomy between work and leisure.

2. The education of adults - from individual demands to collective needs

There have been many attempts to facilitate the acquisition of additional educational qualifications by adults in recent years. Diversification in the higher education sector, for instance, has brought about an increase in 'mature students', whose professional experience may be recognized as a substitute for educational qualifications for the purpose of admission to a specific course.

The problems presented by studying while working have led to the development of modular courses and qualifications, the expansion of correspondence courses and to spectacular initiatives in the field of distance education, such as the Open University in the United Kingdom. The justification and precondition for this approach to continuing education are individual motivation and demand.

The changing economic and demographic situation is, however, increasingly affecting teaching. In their search for new support to attain their objectives, a number of establishments, in particular universities, have recently attempted an opening towards the needs of the local community. Furthermore, the measures taken in the non-university area of adult education have increasingly been related to the demands of a specific public, such as housewives wishing to take up employment again, or retired people.

The credibility of adult education as a national policy instrument has in many countries been hampered by the fact that its most dynamic elements are to be found among private and voluntary organizations. Yet it is precisely these groups who have been many of the first to tackle the problem of attracting the less motivated, more disadvantaged sections of the population.

The vitality and sensitivity demonstrated at local level has contributed to a growing awareness in official circles, in many member countries, that a more comprehensive policy of continuing education is required. The structure of public funding, the identification of target groups and collective needs, the educational methodology appropriate to the adult learner, the training and status of teachers all became the subject of many official enquiries and new national policy guidelines.

However, the new plans and proposals in this area have not sufficed to bridge the gulf between adult education and vocational training, nor to demonstrate the relevance of adult education to the immediate needs of the labour market in particular. Hence the tendency to make it a prime target for budget cuts.

3. Continuing vocational training - from labour market demands to individual needs

Vocational training and re-training had already become an area of government intervention during the period of economic growth, primarily in order to improve the operating capacity and flexibility of the economy and to ensure the re-adaptation of workers from declining industries for employment in growth sectors. Continuing vocational training - in terms of the so-called manpower approach - is designed to influence the quality of the supply of labour, acting as a lubricant in an essentially self-adjusting mechanism of supply and demand for labour in the primary labour market. The manpower approach continues to dominate most of the new programmes for re-training unemployed workers developed since the beginning of the economic recession.

In areas of high unemployment, the function of vocational training is, however, no longer that of solving a problem of mismatch between the demand and supply for labour. It has in many respects become a means of distorting 'free' competition: at one extreme, it can provide a form of hidden subsidy to the few firms considering new industrial investment in regional priority areas. At the other extreme, it can provide a response to those of the unemployed who are individually motivated to better their qualifications, in the hope of increasing their ability to compete in a shrinking labour market. These are the 'mature students' of vocational training.

Insufficient consideration has hitherto been given to the potential of continuing vocational training, in conjunction with other instruments, such as fiscal policy, in promoting a demand for labour, or stimulating job creation, for example by training in managerial skills. The content of training and the structure of qualifications have nevertheless been better and better adapted to the changing content of jobs. Whilst consistent with the 'manpower' approach, such an adaptation has led to a greater emphasis on the need for a versatile and flexible labour force. The importance of qualities such as independence, judgement and initiative having been stressed, the training sector has tended to focus on the individual learning process, placing stress more on structured work experience than on formal instruction.

Nowhere has this trend been more evident than in the development of initial training measures for young people.

4. Young people: towards a synthesis

Education and manpower authorities have been brought together in unprecedented forms of cooperation, thanks to a massive injection of financial resources for education, training and job creation to combat youth unemployment.

It is within this context that there has been a new understanding of the type of basic qualifications needed to cope with adult life in a changing society, an appreciation of the variety of effective learning situations, related to life experience as opposed to formal instruction and a recognition of the need for the kind of vocational guidance which takes account of individual needs and aspirations.

Thanks to these efforts focusing on the initial period of apprenticeship for life, some of the old dialectic between education and training has been overcome. Moreover, in many of the job creation programmes and training workshops for young people, a completely new relationship with the local community has been established. Links between the needs of young people and the needs of the local community have begun to emerge. However, little of this experience has been systematized. At national level, this experience has not been applied to other age groups. The period between the age of 16 and 19 is still generally considered to be a period of transition from learning to earning.

5. <u>Dynamism at the periphery</u>

The experience of youth unemployment schemes can, however, shed a new light on a number of other 'social action' initiatives being carried out at local level. Some are explicitly educational, others to do more with social welfare, the organization of cultural activities, the revival of rural crafts, environmental protection, consumer cooperatives, etc. Insofar as they involve people in new activities, for which they have little formal preparation, they imply a process of continuing education - with the specific objective of assisting an individual to influence his/her environment.

Achievements have been highly diverse. Classifications can be made according to the groups directly involved (e.g. the homeless, the unemployed, parents), the initial aims of the activity (e.g. provision of new services, new educational facilities, new forms of employment, new forms of participation and control in decision-making) or again according to the systems of financing (e.g. sale of products or services, self-financing, public subsidies from national or local sources, support from private sources, finance for 'action research').

The trend towards 'social self-organization' [1] can be
seen as a sign of the cultural vitality of an advanced
industrial society. It can also be seen as a conscious
attempt to create the social fabric necessary to withstand negative changes, to counteract depopulation,
for instance, or to promote solidarity in a local community.

In most cases, difficulties can be traced back to a
specific problem in the local environment - as dramatic
as delinquency in new towns, racial tensions in inner-city
areas, mass redundancies in mono-industrial communities,
or as banal as the lack of coordination between existing
plans and services. Also, there too often exists a
tendency to look at "local action" of this kind from a
sectoral angle. Whereas in educational circles attention
is focused on the new educational "districts", the "open
school", on information at local level concerning what is
available educationally and on the introduction of multimedia, combining radio or television with local backup
services, there is more interest from the employment
policy angle, in re-training and putting back to work
workers who have been made redundant, in the revival of
production cooperatives, the development of small and
medium-sized firms, the evaluation of job creation
programmes and in extending the "informal" economy.
Concertation at local level, in response to a local
problem, can bring about a new willingness to overcome
the administrative constraints, in particular, of
national sectoral policies and may be a vital factor
in the promotion of regional development.

---

[1] Report on the Study Group on the new characteristics of
socio-economic development. European Commission (DG II),
Brussels, December 1977.

6. The use of time

The central problem of providing individuals with the means
to participate in continuing education has not been
resolved. This question has been conspicuous by its
absence in discussions on the employment crisis where
attention has focused more on adjusting working hours
than on re-distributing periods of "non-work".
The concept of paid leave for employees to complete
their training was nevertheless an important issue in
collective agreements and national policies for the
improvement of working conditions, with the ratification
of the ILO Convention No. 140 becoming a useful tool
in bargaining at national level. It can be acknowledged
that major developments have taken place, whilst
admitting the shortcomings of most schemes of paid
eudcational leave, which tend to limit opportunities
to strictly vocational or strictly trade union
objectives, and which inevitably tend to benefit the
most articulate, motivated and integrated members of
the work force.

The question which now arises, is whether a system
of intermittent leave, funded primarily by the employers
and limited to those fortunate workers with secure
employment, holds out real prospects as a strategy
for developing continuing education.

In some countries there are pressures to shift the
financial responsibility for paid educational leave for
workers on to society as a whole. There is also a growing
demand that the right of educational leave be extended
to self-employed workers and to the "non-active" sections
of the population. The idea of a universal, deferable

"drawing right", with appropriate income support, for all forms of post-compulsory education and training has been the central motto and creed of the prophets of continuing education. In spite of much detailed work on this issue, particularly by the OECD, there are few signs of any serious consideration being given by policy makers to its implementation at national level

III. TOWARDS A MORE INTEGRATED STRATEGY

1. A new scenario

One of the most serious characteristics of the present situation is the growing lack of confidence in society's capacity to deal with its problems, to resolve tensions and to establish a strategy of adaptation.

The most immediate problem of unemployment was precipitated by the energy crisis, which is only one feature of the gradual redistribution of economic power between the rich industrialized countries and certain poorer third world countries. The impact of new technologies, of which microelectronics is currently the most significant, introduces further elements of uncertainty and will intensify the process of social as well as economic change. It is known that these factors will necessarily involve a steady increase in the amount of non-working time available to our society.

Whereas most existing policy instruments are attuned only to the negative concept of unemployment or alternatively to the purely recreational aspect of leisure, these trends coincide with and reinforce the emerging demands of some sections of society for different patterns of economic growth which place greater stress on qualitative goals and highlight new priorities in the use of time, space and resources. These aspirations can also be seen in the context of demographic trends and the pressures for equal treatment of the sexes.

The underlying problems of inequality in society, for which economic growth was for so long held out as a panacea, have meanwhile been exacerbated. New inequalities - between age groups, or between the public and private sector - are adding to the unresolved tensions caused by factors such as economic inequality, regional disparities, sex stereotyping and racial prejudice. There can be discerned today a dangerous and wasteful polarization within Western society between those who have the resources and opportunities for participation in the workings of society, whatever their actual level of income, and those who are being increasingly pushed to the fringe of society through job insecurity, enforced inactivity, and a lack of basic education. The gradual adaptation of existing policies to take account of these unresolved issues will demand a more explicit intersectoral approach. For the purpose of this paper, particular stress can be placed on the challenges presented by the problems of the distribution of working and non-working time, and by the concept of social and economic development.

2. The distribution of time

It must be assumed that there will be, within the European Community - as much in the interests of efficiency as for the sake of social justice and democratization of the decision-making process - a positive commitment to the goal of achieving opportunities and greater participation in the development of society by its citizens. In the present situation, this necessarily implies an attempt to redistribute opportunities for work, leisure and education and training.

A strategy for redistribution can be devised through a policy of 'time-budgeting' - the allocation to all citizens of a certain credit in terms of time and income to be used in different ways, for educational or leisure activities or for early retirement.

Such a strategy on the use of time cannot be handled exclusively in the traditional context of paid educational leave (see II 6 above) since its implications go much wider. A system of 'sabbatical' leave could help to eliminate the stigma of unemployment and redistribute leisure time in response to both individual and collective needs. It could provide a means of reintroducing labour market mobility and flexibility, promoting innovation, ventures into self-management and job creation; it could boost the 'remedial' activities of adult education, and provide for the acquisition of new skills; it could ease the conflicts faced by working parents and generally enable people to plan their activities and control their own use of time.

These wider implications need to be discussed and understood by all the agents concerned. The financial implications can only be considered from a comprehensive point of view, taking account of income policies, social security provisions, educational and training investments, etc. Such a policy might require only a redistribution of resources rather than an allocation of new resources. It would, however, demand a new degree of solidarity and flexibility in the organization of work. In various countries and in particular industrial sectors, considerable experience already exists with regard to measures as diverse as maternity or parental leave, systems of flexible retirement as well as in the field of educational leave.

3. **The concept of social and economic development**

   An equally ambitious challenge is presented by the need to adapt policies for economic and social development to take greater account of the human element: the involvement of the individual citizen in improving his social and economic environment and, in particular, in responding to the needs of local communities. The emphasis having for a long time been placed, in macro-political terms, on the 'welfare society' and the reliance on economic growth as the key to development, the local and regional dimension has only comparatively recently been introduced into sectoral policies. These were primarily concerned hitherto with the overall management of the primary labour market, with the general restructuring of specific branches of industry or agriculture, or with the devising of measures on a national scale for broad target groups such as young people, migrants or the elderly.

   In various countries a trend towards a decentralization of responsibility, at least as regards policy implementation, has emerged in specific sectors in the interests of greater efficiency and in order to respond to the demands for participation by those directly concerned. Continuing education can play an important role in this respect. In the first instance, there is a need to identify and promote the conditions under which it will be able to make an effective impact on local and regional development, in particular via the acquisition of self-management techniques. It is in this context that it will be up to the European Community to promote innovation and local initiatives by encouraging debate and stimulating the exchange of experience.

IV. A ROLE FOR THE EUROPEAN COMMUNITY

1. The prospects opened up by the second enlargement of the Community

With the second enlargement of the European Community, which began with the entry of Greece in January 1981, the sudden widening of disparities between the regions and Member States of the Community - in terms of per capita income, industrial development, levels of education, basic social infrastructure, etc. - will undoubtedly provide a considerable challenge to its internal cohesion. It is important that a greater regional dimension should be introduced in many policies conducted at Community level, that is, a greater recognition than hitherto of the need for differentiated measures according to different stages of development.

Measures at Community level have hitherto largely reflected the norms of development established in the more industrialized Member States. There will soon, however, be at least five Member States in a Community of twelve, each with a significant rural sector, both in terms of working population and of area. In varying degrees, the rural sector of these countries may be characterized by an unstructured labour force (seasonal and family work), under-employment, a drift from the country to the town and illiteracy, but also by its strong-cultural traditions.

It is in the context of social and economic development strategies for disadvantaged rural areas that the potential role of continuing education can be best illustrated. Financial intervention in such areas can rapidly reach the limits of its effectiveness if the rural communities themselves are not ready to participate in a process of change.

It is essential, therefore, that continuing education campaigns, particularly the arousing of interest in such education, accompany new forms of employment and self-generated job creation (for instance, by cooperative enterprises, in local crafts, agricultural processing or provision of tourist facilities), on which depends the survival of these rural communities.

2. A number of starting points

For this paper, three specific themes are suggested as starting points for reflection with regard to a strategy of action at Community level in the field of continuing education. Each theme demonstrates the inter-relationship between education and training and the importance of providing guidance and counselling for adults throughout their lives. In different ways the three themes raise questions about the concept of work and the misleading distinction between individual and collective needs. They focus on particular objectives that may be attained most effectively by coordinated action at local level.

(i) The problem of basic adult education and literacy

The most striking characteristic of the problem of adult illiteracy is that, in so far as the problem has been recognized, it has led to some of the most innovative examples of continuing education. There has been significant progress, in mobilizing non-traditional educational resources (e.g. job creation schemes) and new learning situations (e.g. cooperative enterprises and child care centres) and devising new links between the measures taken at national level (e.g. the mass media) and local initiatives.

Only a few urbanized countries such as the
United Kingdom and the Netherlands acknowledge
the problem of adult illiteracy as a national
priority in the field of adult education. The
existence of this phenomenon means at the very
least that more thorough-going comparative
research should be carried out. Given the high
rates of illiteracy in certain rural areas,
particularly in the southern part of the enlarged
Community, the links between basic adult education
and economic development can no longer be
neglected at Community level.

Illiteracy, with all the stigma that is attached
to the notion and the rather limited scholastic
definition that it implies, is no longer appropriate
as a concept in a rapidly changing society.
Basic competences such as have been promoted in
many programmes for the young unemployed, may
provide notions, which are more useful and which
are applicable to the needs of many older adults.
The extension of basic adult education provisions
with a view to promoting basic skills is
particularly relevant in a Community which needs
to be made 'technologically literate' in the
age of microelectronics.

(ii) Continuing education and training as a preparation for new forms of work and development

Closely linked to the notion of 'survival skills'
is the notion of entrepreneurial skills,
traditionally associated with the formal training
of management personnel for small and medium
sized enterprises. Neither initial education nor

vocational training provisions have been geared generally to the acquisition of such skills. However the substantial job creation potential in the secondary labour market and in alternative small-scale forms of employment is now beginning to be recognized as an important factor in the readjustment of the labour market at local level.

There is a clear need for continuing education and training to become more responsive to these trends and to take an active role in promoting "spontaneous" job creation, taking the form of cooperatives, self-employment, shared work, and so on. This need not be limited to the provision of technical support for ready-made projects, whose economic viability is checked beforehand, and full commitment is assumed.

Education and training as an instrument of social and economic development policy at regional and local level may aim more generally to make job creation feasible by encouraging a collective spirit of innovation and dynamism and by promoting group work on the preparation of projects. The setting up of a cooperative work project provides in itself a vehicle for learning.

There is already a proliferation of examples of self-organization in economic activities in many countries, sometimes forming part of the domestic non-market economy, or being linked to 'social utility' schemes, rather than being seen as productive enterprises in the classical sense of the term. Frequently, training in self-management skills is implicit rather than explicit. If wider encouragement is to be given to these forms of job creation, more flexibility will thus be required in the criteria used by the financial support machinery for continuing education and training.

(iii) <u>Older workers and the transition to retirement</u>

The social importance attached to paid employment lingers on in the traditional work ethic of Western societies. It can have a particularly harsh effect on older citizens, who in retirement may be cut off from their principal means of human contact and social participation. Throughout the Community, given demographic projections and the present trend towards earlier retirement, there will be increasing numbers of fit and active older people facing a long stretch of more or less enforced inactivity. Moreover, it is often those who have benefited least from the education system while young and who have had least opportunity for creative leisure time during working life who are now finding themselves in prolonged unemployment or premature retirement.

The social issues involved are all the more significant in the light of the relative absence of coordinated policies on the transition to retirement in any way comparable to the analysis and investment devoted to the transition of young people to working life. However, following the same logic, similar provisions may usefully be made for older workers : phased transition, alternating periods of work and rest; continuing systems of guidance and counselling in preparation

for post-retirement occupations; the development
of basic skills, not in the traditional terms of
health care and pension rights, but in the sense
of social self-organization. The talents,
energies and experience of the mass of older
people should not be lost to society, especially since
certain outstanding senior personalities are
venerated until they die.
The focus on the period of transition to retirement
illustrates most clearly the need for collaborative
efforts between individual firms and local
communities. There is wide scope for innovation
in this area.

3. The potential of existing instruments

(i) Community activity in the field of continuing
education has been marked by the explicit sectoral
approach of the founding Treaties, which provide
separate instruments for training measures in the
coal and steel industry, in agriculture and
in certain aspects of employment policy. The
educational and regional aspects, among other things,
were left implicit in the preamble of the
Rome Treaty. The general principles for the
implementation of a common policy on vocational
training established in 1963,[1] together with
the general guidelines agreed in 1971[2] reflect
the hypotheses of the period concerning economic
growth, but nevertheless provide a useful basis for
cooperative action. They stress the need for
inter-sectoral coordination, the adaptation of
structures to changing economic and social
circumstances and the inter-linkage between

---

(1) OJ 63, 20.4.1963.
(2) OJ C 81, 12.8.1971.   See also the Council conclusions
of 26.11.1970 on the problems of adult education as an
instrument of an active employment policy.

education and training. Similar objectives were again proposed in a different economic context by the joint Council of Ministers for the Economy, Finance and Social Affairs at its meeting in Luxembourg on 11 June 1981.

(ii) The European Social Fund, which is the principal Community financial instrument in this field, has proved flexible in adapting its priorities according to trends in the employment situation. Although traditionally concerned with the 'manpower approach' to vocational training, with an emphasis on re-training of the unemployed, an illustration of the Fund's potential was the introduction of new types of aid for young people in 1979.[1] The intention to finance 'demonstration projects' in programmes of alternating work and training for young people may herald a stage in which the Social Fund can move more explicitly towards a concept of continuing education, particularly for those in marginal jobs and whose basic education is deficient.

The Social Fund pilot projects offer the most flexibility to promote examples of integrated local development projects, both in urban and rural areas, cutting across the boundaries of the main fields of intervention.

---

(1) OJ L 361, 23.12.1978.
(2) OJ C 1, 3.1.1980.

Within the context of the Fund's sectoral intervention, e.g. programmes for workers leaving agriculture, for women or for the unemployed in regional priority areas, a few schemes have already been adopted explicitly concerning rural development or involving management training for the creation of cooperatives.

(iii) The policy pursued by the Community in specific economic sectors also places emphasis on the social implications at local or individual level. In the agricultural sector, for instance, it is mandatory [1] on Member States to provide an advisory service to help farmers and their families, whose farm is no longer adapted to modern agriculture, solve their socio-economic problems. In the coal and steel sector, the promotion of alternative employment and appropriate training for redundant workers has been one of the principal axes of the ECSC Treaty. At a time of economic recession, sectoral instruments of this nature risk entering into competition with each other unless counselling and vocational guidance structures are coordinated at local level.

(iv) The Commission guidelines on flexible retirement [2] raise the issue of 'non-work' from the point of view both of the economic situation (in the context of work-sharing) and of the individual. This pinpoints the merits of systems of phased retirement - "to avoid an abrupt changeover from full-time work to complete idleness, with the potentially disastrous consequences of a sudden acceleration of ageing ...".[3] In this context,

---

(1) Directive 72/161/EEC Title I.
(2) COM(80) 393 final of 14.7.80
(3) Op.cit. page 8

it examines, inter alia, the ways in which loss of earnings through shorter working hours may be compensated by schemes financed from public funds.

Apart from having direct relevance to the policy for re-structuring specific sectors of the economy, these considerations could be seen in the much wider context of educational leave and of "crédits d'heures" (time off for educational purposes) applicable to all members of the work force at any stage of their career.

Tripartite bodies, such as the Standing Committee on Employment, could pursue the debate on work-sharing from this perspective and ultimately consider the possible use of Community legal instruments to provide for the redistribution of work and a simplified system of allowances for "non-work" time, financed from public funds. Future orientations governing aid allocation, particularly from the Social Fund could be important in this respect.

(v) An explicitly intersectoral approach is being adopted at Community level, and within Member States, to the introduction of new information technologies.[1] A basic familiarity with, and understanding of microelectronics, particularly regarding their application to daily tasks at work and in the home, will be

---

(1) cf. European Society faced with the challenge of the new information technologies (COM(79)650). Employment and the new microelectronic technology (COM(80)16).

required at every level of society and among all age groups. These massive learning needs cut across the education/training divide, across individual and collective requirements, and across different generations and socio-economic groups. Given the scarce resources, at least as regards software and expertise among educators, schools and universities will be able to develop a wider educational role, sharing their resources with the local community and local industry, setting up programmes in conjunction with the mass media which cater for young and old together, for those in work and out of work.

(vi) The key to an intersectoral strategy for social and economic development and the coordination of financial instruments at Community level could well emerge in the context of regional policy; it appears all the more likely with the prospect of a second enlargement of the Community (see Section IV.1).

At present the regional development programmes of Member States, supported by the European Regional Development Fund, pay scarce attention to the social and educational aspects of regional policy.[1]

---

(1) Outlines for Regional Development Programmes (OJ C 69, 24.3.76) and the Commission Opinion of 23.5.1979 (OJ L 143, 12.6.79).

A new perspective has however been opened by the non-quota section of this Fund, since this section gives more explicit recognition to the need "to fix clear-cut aims, no longer by Community aid to individual projects financed by Member States, but by overall programmes, which correspond to the economic requirements of the region and are of a nature to create conditions for their self-development". Within the framework of such overall programmes, but at local as well as regional level, differing sectoral needs can be reconciled and the contribution provided by continuing education and training can be integrated.

4. Systems of interaction

The adaptation of sectoral policies and their financial mechanisms is necessarily slow and complex. It is necessary, however, to encourage continuing discussion and reform on an intersectoral basis, taking full account of the increased size of the rural sector in an enlarged Community.

An important but often underestimated stimulus to innovation can come from below, in particular via an exchange of experience on the various integrated programmes that already exist. Some such programmes have already been documented in comparative form at international or European level.[1] The exchange of experience between certain categories of educators and local development agents could be developed along the lines of the study visit programmes already implemented at Community level in the field of higher education.

---
(1) cf. as examples, the CEDEFOP file on Innovations in Continuing Education and Training and the CEDEFOP studies in France, Italy and the United Kingdom on the Role of Training in the Creation of New Social and Economic Activities; also the interaction networks on Adult and Permanent Education of the Council of Europe.

The new measures for promoting residential adult education, proposed for 1982, could also be oriented so as to support visit programmes enabling persons in charge of local community projects to inspect comparable projects initiated in other Member States.

Carefully monitored research can also have wide repercussions on the development of national policies and in stimulating other similar projects.[1] Multinational research networks could be developed in respect of local counselling and information centres, the training of teachers or basic adult education.

---

[1] cf. Pilot projects on poverty and on the transition from education to working life.

5.
Closing speech by

Mr Jacques Delors
Director of the Research Centre 'Work and Society',
University of Paris IX Dauphine.
In October 1980, Mr Delors was a Member of the European Parliament and Chairman of its Committee for Economic and Monetary Affairs.
Since May 1981, he has been Minister for Economic Affairs and Finance in France

XII/49/81-EN

POINTERS FOR CONTINUING EDUCATION IN EUROPE
Jacques Delors
SEMINAR ON NEW PERSPECTIVES FOR CONTINUING EDUCATION AND
TRAINING, BERLIN, 14-17 OCTOBER 1980

At a time when the European Community is going through one of the most serious crises in its history, it might seem unrealistic to consider extending its activities to areas not explicitly covered by the Treaty of Rome.

Education is one of those areas. Yet, this seminar on continuing training is timely. While grappling with far reaching economic changes, all the member countries are questioning the aims, successes and failures of what in the 1960s was regarded as one of the primary vehicles for social change: training extended to all stages of an individual's life.

Accordingly, a rigorous assessment must be made of the present situation at national and Community level before attempting to give fresh impetus to continuing education.

First, it is as well to recall the precise aims of continuing education policy:
- to enable each one to tackle the multiple problems arising in working life;
- to combat inequality of opportunity;
- apart from working life, in the context of life in general, to achieve more control over everyday existence and improve the quality of life, that is, give more depth to the individual's cultural development in the broadest sense, to enable him to cope with all the problems that arise in private life and social relations.

First, I would like to dwell a moment on the reasons for the disappointment now felt in regard to education compared with the high hopes in the 1960s. You may perhaps remember President Johnson's words: "The answer for all national problems comes to the single word: education". At that time the OECD and other international organizations believed in education in a society enjoying strong and steady economic growth as a means of facing the future and as a panacea for many current problems. Compared with the enthusiasm of the 1960s, there would appear to be a general feeling of disillusion and I would like to go over the main reasons. Present awareness of these reasons will spare us a good many errors in the future.

The educational system did not know how to, or could not, answer the challenges facing it. The challenges have not gone away: they are arising again, and constitute the main hurdle to be surmounted in our thinking - whether at theoretical or practical level - about education policies.

The potential contribution of Community initiatives in the field of education should be viewed in the light of this overall context. I will venture to formulate a few ideas to be kicked around in the forthcoming debate.

1. REASONS FOR WIDESPREAD DISAPPOINTMENT

Why have the hopes of the 1960s come to nothing? To understand this, we should remember firstly how much was expected of education at that time, and secondly the clash between the educational system and a society undergoing radical change: for although the first oil price rise was a landmark in history, I reckon that the crisis in European industrial society had already begun at the end of the 1960s. From that time, disappointment with progress became manifest as did the limits of continuing education and training policies.

Expectations with respect to education

To go straight to the heart of the matter, I would recall that the two main expectations were linked on the one side with the emergence of mass education due to demographic growth and the raising of the school-leaving age combined with a spontaneous demand for education - and on the other, the belief that the education system could act as a factor of economic and social change.

Most education systems failed to provide adequate education for the masses. I shall say no more. The seminar has elected to set up a working party on illiteracy. I, for one, have seen (and Anna Lorenzetto bore eloquent witness to this in her report) the failures for which the education system could be held accountable in our society: social misfits, marginalization, new forms of inequality - all due to the failure of the education system to provide adequate mass education.

As for education as a factor of economic and social change, you will probably recall the argument between the militants in the academic world, the avant garde claiming that society must first be reformed then education can be changed, and the political militants claiming that if education is reformed society will change. It is a question, if I may say so, of the chicken and the egg, and I will not pronounce on it. I am merely noting that a feeling of disappointment exists.

Coming now to the question of continuing education proper, and considering experience overall, I think it is not too much to say that continuing education and training have fulfilled their adaptive function fairly well. In places where continuing training has been developed in the last 10 years economic results have been better, for the labour force was flexible enough to adapt fairly quickly to new production conditions, new forms of work organization. With respect to the more ambitious goals of job mobility and social mobility, the continuing education programmes cannot on balance be said to have been a success. Why is this? Has the crisis masked the problem and pushed concerns about continuing training into the background? I cannot contain a certain feeling of impatience when I hear the serious problems facing us today casually dismissed with: "How can you regard continuing education as the top priority nowadays? Heads of firms and trade unions are mainly concerned with competitivity and employment and continuing education has to take a back seat." The other reaction is: "When we were in a period of strong growth, continuing education was a good idea for times of prosperity but not in times of economic recession." I reject both these views categorically. If they were true, it would mean that the hopes placed in education in the

1960s were linked to a short span of 30 years when the industrial societies in Europe were carried away by a form of euphoria - the idea of unlimited growth. This does not reflect the fact that educational problems are just as meaningful in a society which must adapt, must change.. or give up.

Encounter with a society undergoing radical change

I will consider the subject from the point of view of the obstacles and will not dwell long on the main aspects of this change. I have already pointed out that the rise in the price of oil was merely one factor in what was a much richer, more complex and more distressing historical sequence. The educational system in general was faced by three main changes which created hitherto unresolved problems: the compartmentalization of knowledge, haphazard consumption of information related to the proliferation of the mass media, and lastly, certain employment problems that became very evident from the mid-1960s and were linked to a crisis in the employer/worker relationship, even in socially advanced societies like Sweden and Norway. Those are the three problems facing education and consequently the culture of our time.

First, let me deal with the phenomenon of compartmentalized knowledge. In her opening remarks Shirley Williams underlined the difficulties facing men and women in a computerized society dependent on symbols and changing more and more rapidly. In these conditions a person with highly specialized knowledge, even of a high standard, is not equipped to respond to the challenge. This is one of the main defects of the education system, which, in fact, is related to society's basic culture. Too much weight has been given to novelty at the expense of knowledge accumulated over time. Education concerns the accumulated capital of knowledge about themselves acquired by generation after generation. If the fund of transmitted knowledge is displaced by novelty, there is a danger that the immediate and the ephemeral will be regarded as the essential and that society as a whole will lose the ability to see itself and historical change in perspective.

This is why in countries where a sharp distinction is made between general education and vocational training, the lack of general education of a good standard will constitute an ever greater handicap. This is why in countries like France where general education is given preference over vocational training, this approach must be maintained so that men or women in the 1980s and 1990s will, through their reading of past history, be able to determine their own means of action and fulfil their responsibilities.

The haphazard consumption of information tends in the same direction. When in the space of a quarter of an hour 20 or more events are presented on television, how can children assimilate them, place them in some order, integrate them into their understanding of the world? This calls for perspective and learning. Where continuing education and education in general are concerned, it would be a mistake to say that they are losing ground, for they are without doubt the only comprehensive response to these two challenges - compartmentalized knowledge and haphazard consumption of information. This is why education is not a dead letter. To paraphrase a famous revolutionary, I would nearly go as far as saying that it is a new discovery for Europe, for the last 20 years of this century.

Lastly, the third challenge is the crisis in employment which as I said began in the mid-1960s and had both negative and positive aspects. Positive aspects are the aspiration to independence, the rejection of dull work which coincided with the spate of ideas on industrial democracy at that time. Because times are bad it does not mean we should forget this today. Still less should these ideas be forgotten (and I will return to this later) when we consider that the best performing economic systems are those where somehow or other, even if it necessitates a change of heart, the ideas of industrial democracy are applied.

The crisis in employment also had its negative aspects: part of the population became alienated from the work ethic and might even be said to be allergic to work, which led to the distortion of one of the aims of education. What good was learning if it would inevitably lead to an unsatisfying job in a society of which, what is more, the values were rejected. Given the above, it is no wonder that in the last 20 years continuing education and training policies have come up against limits which I will discuss briefly.

Shortcomings of continuing education and training policies

Three phenomena demonstrate the shortcomings of education both as regards content and as a factor of social change: academic failure, the persistence of certain forms of anomie and in recent years the inability to halt the segregation of the labour market.

First I shall deal with the school dropouts. In his report Anthony Kaye points out that 5 to 10% of school-leavers have only the most rudimentary notion of reading, writing and arithmetic. Add to this those who fail to obtain a certificate conferring some degree of employability and the drop-out rate rises to 15-20% per generation in Europe, depending on the country. This is a consequence of the failure by society to assimilate mass education. On the other hand, how could these problems be solved in so short a time? In addition, there is a misconception prevalent among business and management circles to the effect that the education system is a power plant to which the working world has only to hook up for all to be well. In reality, it is not as simple as that:

in modern industrial society after 5 to 10 years only one
person in four is still doing the job for which he or she was
trained. The education system cannot run off qualified persons
like a baker producing bread rolls. It forms men and women for
adulthood, gives them the equipment to solve their problems in
private life or in society and also inculcates the duty to contribute to the common good through work.

Now I come to the second failure of the education system, that
is the persistence of various forms of anomie, illiteracy,
poverty and marginalization. Anna Lorenzetto gave a description
of types of illiteracy which is of great help in understanding
today's problems, particularly recurrent illiteracy where the
acquired skill is not kept up due to an unfavourable environment. Father Eoin Murphy drew attention to the self-perpetuating
aspect of poverty. All these phenomena are present today, yet
in the early 1960s it was supposed that the educational system
would eliminate these elements which bring discredit on our
society.

I now come to the third failure, that is the increasing segregation of the labour market. The education system, in particular continuing education policies, have lost much of their
credibility due to massive and long-term unemployment. At the
beginning of the crisis, countries most advanced in regard
to adult education gave those who were out of work training
for six months, nine months, one year.

The continuing training course required a personal effort on
the part of the persons concerned and was to give them an
opportunity to re-enter the working world. This idea, however,
has been gradually eroded in Europe since hundreds of thousands
of young people or adult workers found they had been shunted off
to dead-end training course ("formation-parking").

This accordingly lowered the credibility of continuing training. For many the segregation of the labour market is a reality. Today, there is a central market in which the workers are protected: very well in the public service, relatively well under collective agreements. Then there are those on the fringe who represent 5 to 15% of the working population in our countries and who are condemned to low wages, forced mobility, precarious employment conditions. I am well aware that some have opted for insecurity but let us not lose sight of the wood for the trees. For every one who prefers to work for a temporary employment agency rather than have a steady job, there are nine who are forced to endure fixed-term contracts and lack of security. The latter can expect little aid from current training policy. These three points could account for some of the disappointment currently felt regarding continuing education and training.

2. CHALLENGES FACING THE EDUCATION SYSTEM

These challenges directly reflect the prevailing disillusioned view of education. First, there are the consequences of the demographic and financial situation on which I shall not dwell as they have already been talked of at length. Equal opportunity should continue to be given high priority in the education system, bearing in mind the failures I have just pointed out. Then we come to the fundamental question: how can the education system help European societies to control the changes taking place and point the way to a new model for development that will fulfil our aspirations while keeping within the bounds imposed by economic constraints?

Consequences of the demographic and financial situation

I will just mention these in passing as Professor Javeau has already given us a remarkable analysis. As the Professor noted, retirement is a social phenomenon. He showed how the rush towards early retirement measures as the only solution to the problems of industrial restructuring was open to doubt and was indeed very questionable. Mr Faulkner's report also underlined the seriousness and difficulty of the problems connected with the transition from working life to retirement in a rapidly changing society, and one that places a premium on competitiveness and youth. Professor Javeau observed that the main question was to determine the potential social usefulness of persons in retirement.

I would point out that even in countries where the birthrate has fallen - this has not occurred in all European countries the number of young people encountering difficulties at school is on the increase. This is not the only paradox in the present situation. Lastly, the financial stumbling block should not be forgotten. There is unlikely to be any great increase in resources allocated to education in our countries in the years to come. Resources must therefore be redeployed. This situation should serve as the backcloth to our discussions.

Equality of opportunity as a top priority

We have discussed certain factors, such as the impact of massive unemployment and the segregation of the labour market, and now I would like to draw your attention to a more pervasive danger looming over industrial society: I refer to the collapse of the unity of purpose implicit in social welfare policies. Apart from Germany and Austria, everywhere the level of social protection built up under the Welfare State is being more or less rapidly eroded, with a consequent increase in inequalities. The Welfare State was based on a simple idea - universal entitlement - or, as Olof Palme put it: "Society should be kinder to the weak and more demanding of the strong." Today this view is contested and the education system cannot simply turn its back on the issue.

Will the education system help to prevent this regression, or will it succumb to this wave of renewed attacks on social welfare policies?

This brings us to three issues as old as the hills that need to be approached with frankness and intellectual rigour.

The first is the age-old argument about inborn and acquired skills, in view of the strong swing back to the heredity theory. The second concerns access to employment for everyone - a philosophy that regards work as central to society - and the last is the ultimate ambition of education policy - the individual's ability to master the problems of existence.

With respect to the eternal debate concerning acquired and innate skills, the reports by Anna Lorenzetto, Father Murphy and Anthony Kaye speak for themselves. There can be no equality of opportunity unless account is taken of the individual's social environment. In our society language is the passport to success, particularly in school; the desire to learn varies considerably depending on social category. By desire to learn, I mean motivation. For example, in France, in the poorer social strata children in the 14 to 16 age group are pressed to leave school early. This is not mere chance but the consequence of necessity. I am not going to pronounce on the vexed question of acquired and inborn skills, but I would ask those in favour of retracing their footsteps who are leading the counter-offensive to look at the facts, be sufficiently honest to examine what happens, and admit that most problems of marginalization and "new" poverty are due to failure at school and a deprived environment.

The second point - employability

Employability is a difficult concept for it embraces subjective and objective parameters. The subjective parameter is the desire to work in a certain job, and the objective parameter is the ability to fill the post. I am firmly convinced that it is a mistake to regard employability from the purely objective point of view. Even with massive unemployment, employability in our society continues to be an essential preliminary in the fight against inequality of opportunity. André Boutin's report covered three main areas whose importance cannot be overstated. In the first place, thought should be given to the organization of the transition from school to work between 16 and 20 years. Since, if you will pardon the expression, the school cannot turn out "finished products" and since young people mature early, the way must be paved for adolescents to come face to face with society and working life between the ages of 16 and 20, leaving all avenues open for a return to school or continuing training in parallel with working experience.

Vocational guidance and youth information services could be multiplied but there is no substitute for what young people today consider essential - that is, what they themselves learn from their own confrontation with the working world. Of course, I could enlarge on this point and have already thrown out a lot of ideas, for I regard this problem as vital. I would even say it has a central role in policy as it provides an opportunity for adult society (that has had the benefit of experience of work and economic growth) to show its unity with young people who are naturally disoriented by the situation confronting them.

The second area concerns training/work experience schemes, not only for 16 to 20 year-olds but for everyone. These schemes are a good way, as Shirley Williams wished, of bridging the gap between general education and vocational training without sacrificing either.

The third area concerns community work, which provides a means of training and integration into the working world. My research centre "Travail et Societé" has made a comparative study at European level which has strengthened my beliefs in this area. These projects have proved a positive means of combating unemployment, restoring the self-confidence of the persons concerned, improving employability and even stimulating innovatory social projects. They provide a framework in which young or unemployed persons can take up an activity that suits them and may also be useful to society. In other words, without belittling the education system, the opportunities for learning and socialization have become more diverse in our society, and advantage should be taken of every means towards training and employment. However, in our society progress in this direction will only be possible if the public authorities, trade unions and employers' organi ations regard the education system, the operation of the labour market and the organization of work as a single system in the systems analysis sense or an indissoluble triangle.

Until the dialectical relationship of these three elements is established there is little hope that the education system will correspond to the requirements of working and economic life, and once more become a creative force. Where this triangular relationship does not exist, the result is lack of communication and incomprehension. When I say work organization, I also mean the management of human resources by industry.

Now we come to the third area - the individual's control over his existence. The introductory reports to this seminar have said all there is to say. So many individuals in our society are unaware of their rights! So many do not know how to exercise their rights or find it difficult to fit into society. So many find it difficult to become real citizens even if they so wished - assuming it is so wished at the pinnacles of power (i.e. that the individual should advance beyond the stage of "consume and hold your tongue"). All these matters fall within the domain of continuing education. As you know: the individual's control of his existence cannot be divorced from his control of his working life. They are closely bound together. But you know as well as I do that any high-minded debate about whether or not training should pay off in economic terms ends in a dead-lock. Every time a particular population group must be retrained, the problem of that group's perception of the world must first be considered; this is what Bertrand Schwartz did in his experiment with the iron ore miners at Nancy. He told me that most of the persons concerned had a vocabulary of only 400 words, that their perception of working life was limited to the mine. In these conditions how can individuals be retrained and taught another trade? First their horizons must be expanded and they must be made to realize that their life has not come to an end, their self-confidence must be restored, their perception of society and working live must be enlarged; only then can they usefully follow a vocational training course in the strict sense. This preliminary stage is essential, and there will be increasing cause for concern as the effects of the third industrial revolution are felt. For, let me remind you, in the third revolution, as opposed to the second, the question of how to produce will be more significant than the question of what to produce.

Mastering the transition

Two points are familiar, but I would still like to go over them, perticularly now that the Japanese offensive is front page news. Economic competition does not depend only on up-to-date plant, new production methods or the level of wages and social security contributions. It largely depends on how the basic units are organized. I am not here to praise the Japanese system, but I can tell you that one of the strong points in Japanese productivity is the extraordinary creative ability of the basic unit, its strong links with the other units in the undertaking which enables considerable time to be saved in solving problems, there being no need to summon white collar technicians or halt production. This means that one of the elements in competitivity is the collective ability of the basic work unit to adjust and be inventive, and this is one more justification for continuing training.

More generally speaking, how are we going to live in a computerized society? This too relates to continuing education. It is not only a

question of learning to learn, but a question of unlearning
so that the mind can use new data. Consequently, there is
a certain danger that the computerized society will threaten
individual autonomy and might also devalue general culture.
On the other hand it opens up great possibilities provided
we understand how to use the data and the know-how that
could be made available to us.

This is another aspect of competitivity: how to live and
work in a computerized society are two challenges for education
policy. Now I come to the third area which, I believe, you
discussed in the second working group and which calls for
great optimism and caution. I mean the search for what is
known as a new model for development. In the first place,
I assure you, it is very difficult to sell this idea in
Europe.

The second industrial revolution, the one we have known,
had four main features: mass production, standardization
of goods which led to gains in productivity, concentration
of activities leading to urbanization and, finally, the spread
of Taylorism (scientific management). It has provided consumer
durables for large numbers of people. The third industrial
revolution has great potential if we realize that it could
facilitate the production of more individualized goods and
services, make possible the decentralization of activities
as a result of easy access to information through the new
technology and bring about a new balance between capital
and labour enhancing the latter's quantitative and qualitative
possibilities. Many new jobs could be created in this context

and the jobs themselves would be more rewarding. In this connection, close liaison between innovatory continuing education activities and the search for the new model of development is certainly one of the most positive contributions the educational system could make to the solution of the problems of today and tomorrow. Please do not misunderstand me, I do not mean that the educational system alone can engender the new model of development, but simply that education can perform an integrative and creative function. For instance, society could be organized on the basis of "flexi-time", that is time would no longer be scientifically structured according to Taylor's system, but could in the extreme case be treated as a bank on which people could draw, choosing when to work and when not to. Alternatively, new data processing technology could enhance job content, eliminate dull jobs, or make it possible to decentralize activities. Small basic production units could further the development of new needs, or rather make our contemporaries aware of needs that are important but which have received little attention to date. I would go so far as to say that the central welfare authorities have become excessively bureaucratic and are now finding it difficult to respond to delicate, complex problems such as the integration of elderly persons into working life, training the handicapped, combating anomie or the emergence of new forms of poverty. I am sure that new common bonds forged by a new welfare policy will be based on decentralized units. In this context, training will be closely integrated into the production system; this will certainly open up fruitful paths for education.

3. POINTS FOR EUROPEAN ACTION

In my opening remarks I observed that the Community was going through a very serious intellectual and political crisis, but that the solution did not depend on the outcome of the struggle between federalists and confederalists. Today there must be general agreement on the simple fact that the European industrial societies share a common destiny. They no longer have the benefit of the favourable environment prevailing in the years 1945 to 1972 and are today entering an era when conditions will be much less favourable. Whether it is ascribed to the surge in economic activity throughout the world, the appearance of new competitors, or the 10.-year lag in technology compared with the United States and Japan, the European industrial societies have missed their opportunity and not one of them can hope to survive alone, even the most prosperous.
If a serious social or political crisis were to occur in a European country tomorrow all the others would be affected. Accordingly the thought underlying my proposals is the fact of our common destiny. Given this approach, the question is to what extent could action at Community level intensify national efforts? In other words, to paraphrase the well-known exhortation in the New Testament: Help thyself and Europe will help thee. Therefore Community action should be developed whenever it can underpin national measures but should not be regarded

as a substitute for them. There will be no dispensation from action for the 10 Member States (tomorrow 12), no dispensation for the employers' and trade union associations from undertaking the necessary reorganization. This is the standpoint from which I will set down pointers for Community action.

In the first place, Europe is an ideal centre for the exchange of experience and the promotion of innovation. CEDEFOP could act as a forum for discussion and the dissemination of ideas - all the more necessary since the challenges ahead will call for a great deal of imagination and innovation.

At the same time, care should be taken to adopt a comprehensive rather than a bureaucratic approach to education and training problems in Europe. Naturally, Community officials think in terms of the Social and Regional Funds, EAGGF, etc.; but a broader view of educational problems must be taken, looking beyond those measures. It is up to us to give substance to the political ideas. Once this is done progress can reasonably be expected.

Disseminating innovation

With respect to the exchange of experience and promotion of innovation, the value of which I have already indicated, some of the most interesting projects for which it would be appropriate to set up a pool of documentation concern literacy training, remedial teaching, measures for the 16-20 age group, programmes to integrate the elderly in the life of society and community service schemes. These are five key areas on which the Community should focus and pool experience, while avoiding interdepartmental conflict of interests.

If the Community cannot regularly organize forums for the fruitful exchange of experience what purpose does it serve? It is on the basis of experience that innovation must be encouraged. This leads me to a specific proposal: the Social Fund should allocate some appropriations ex quota to finance innovatory projects directly without going through the national authorities.

Forum for comparison of social problems

I have already criticized the fragmentary nature of Community action and will not revert to this point. The Ministers for Education meet on one side, the Ministers for Labour on another; there is an Employment Committee and a Vocational Training Committee but no general forum for discussion or comparison of social problems commensurate in scope with the questions involved. For some years now first as a trade unionist, then as a civil servant and now as a Member of Parliament - I have been faced with this disappointing state of affairs i.e. it is never possible to be together, for frank discussions, members of the Commission, the Ministers concerned, the trade union and employers' associations without a strict agenda from which each has obstinately deleted all controversial matter. We cannot go on like this; we must recover flexibility and freedom if we are to innovate. We need a forum for discussion - I would not go so far as to say negotiation - on social questions in the Community. We need to share our experience at regular intervals and then I believe we could envisage multiannual programmes covering education, training and employment which should be based on three simple ideas.

First, the importance of action at grass roots level. Reference communities based on the living or work environment could use the school as a community and cultural centre. The grass roots community could be a creative force if the school played the role it should - that is the integrative and creative role I spoke of earlier.

Secondly, where education is concerned much thought should be given to the question of motivation. It is useless to develop programmes without settling this point.

Thirdly, and this will be all the more pertinent in the
enlarged Community, the right to be different must be
respected. There is no sharp dividing line between the
educated and the uneducated. I am horrified that in my country -
and this is not an idle criticism - working class and peasant
culture are so underrated while the synthetic mass culture
put over by the media is given so much weight. In practice
nothing can be constructed, no progress can be made unless
account is taken of the group's own experience. From this
angle, to judge by my personal experience of working class
culture in France, which I helped to develop, it is invaluable.
Even though workers may not master the language which is a
passport to success, they have their own culture and particular
world view. This is a positive advantage on which any progress
or advance must be founded.

Community priorities

Besides experimental and creative programmes, other measures
would seem to be required in the light of the findings of
this meeting and the current requirements of the social
situation in our countries.

First, we have the struggle against illiteracy in its various
forms. I must emphasize the seriousness of recurrent illiteracy
affecting people who left school 20 years earlier poorly
equipped and are faced with the prospect of going back to
school. In my view this problem should be given top priority.

The second area, where Europe cuts a very poor figure,
concerns regions affected by industrial reorganization.
In regions dependent on a single industry - e.g. textiles
or steel - the effect of the crisis on the inhabitants

has been that of a world crumbling about their ears.
It does not simply involve a change of job, or the drama
of dismissal; it represents the collapse of their world.
In these circumstances education and training measures
commensurate with the scale of the problem are needed. Our
research centre has made a study of young unemployed workers
in regions dependent on a single industry - steel or textiles.
We were struck by the fact that for these young people
there was only one career prospect - the father's occupation.
There was only one life style - that of the region where
they were born. And they are attached to that region.

These cases are so dramatic and the problem is so overwhelming
that the Community will lose all credibility if it does not
devote its intellectual abilities, creative capacity and
funds to helping these regions and their inhabitants to find
a new life and new ways of making a living in their own area.

The third priority could be the organization of work. My
earlier remarks about the Japanese way of working and
industrial democracy were not made idly. I am convinced
that tomorrow any non-participatory form of work organization
will result in a loss of productivity of 5 to 10% compared
with situations where worker participation is the rule.
Consequently, thought today about how in a closely linked
system of education, training and work, we can promote
experiments in which the individual has a right to a say
in his own working conditions, and later a right to take
initiatives, is not just a social but an economic necessity
if we are to remain competitive.

The fourth priority could be exploratory work on a new model of development. This task calls for a great deal of thought and imagination, for which I propose that the Social Fund should make an allocation of funds ex quota. The object would not be to construct a full-scale model, but simply to identify, in the "official" and "unofficial" economy in each country, new activities and new job openings corresponding to unsatisfied needs - whether or not training activities were involved.

In other words, what is needed is to encourage risk-takers and disseminate experience acquired which could - by specific example - alleviate the prevailing mood of despondency.

Despondency! This could apply just as well to the prevailing mood in Europe as regards the future of the Community. This is one reason why we should tirelessly put forward proposals for future action, however limited or modest, to dispel this pessimistic outlook and make Europeans realize that at least they share a common destiny.

6. Conclusions and recommendations of the three working groups established during the seminar

6.1. Working group No 1

Report of Group 1: "The development of basic adult education and literacy"

Chairman: Mr C. Snijders

Rapporteur: Father Eoin Murphy

Education as a social system exists in the context of the broader institutional pattern of society. Education must relate to other community, State, private and governmental agencies, each of which has its own characteristics and responsibilities. This group is aware that its consideration of its set topic and the proposals it makes have to be evaluated in interdependence with the philosophical, political and economic values of society. Two themes based on these values are the objects of discussion by other groups and we constantly imply the connection between these three themes and, on occasion, explicitly state it.

Education for living and education as a preparation for work have long been accepted as parallel and complementary aims for the educational institutions of society. It is disturbing to see, then, that in the Member States of the EEC, and in those States who will join in the near future, there exists a significant number of people, who have achieved minimal success as measured either by their preparedness for work or by their ability to participate in the everyday life of our societies. They usually have little experience of vocational preparation, and are most likely to secure types of employment which also offer no opportunities for retraining or for personal development. A marked lack of motivation towards work and further study make these people incapable of adapting to changing circumstances and they tend to develop into the long-term unemployed, fostering a cycle of economic and cultural poverty in their own families and in their communities.

We are convinced that the Member States must recognize that there are people in all our countries who are illiterate, gravely disadvantaged and economically unproductive because of complex environmental, social and educational deprivation. It is important to note that these groups are not only migrant workers, but members of the indigenous population who have grown up in their native culture. It is necessary that the European Community, with its commitment to improving the social conditions of people in its Member States, faces this problem so fundamental to its existence and applies appropriate effort and resources to remedying it. In the Community document "Towards a European education policy", it is stated that "the road to true equality of opportunity is a long one and it will take more than statements of policy, however generous, to eliminate the obstacles that still face poor or handicapped children". The Ministers will recognize, as will their education and social planners, that motivation in the home and positive attitudes towards education in a local community are vital factors in helping under-privileged children to achieve a rightful place in society.

All the governments in Member States are faced with
economic stringencies at the present moment, and in
times of recession the first to suffer are the under-
privileged and disadvantaged in our societies. In a
time of plenty, humane interest for the handicapped
may be observable to all and portrayed as a Community
problem, but in times of economic or political crisis
the Community's ability to observe the needs of the
handicapped may be repressed and denied. The European
Community must beware of falling into that trap if
it is to remain credible in the eyes of the many
politically aware people in member countries who are
becoming increasingly aware of the plight of disadvantaged
people and in the eyes of the disadvantaged groups
themselves who are growing more frustrated and
alienated from the objectives of the European Community.

For this reason, we put forward proposals which involve
reallocation of resources. We do this in the firm conviction
that economic considerations and administrative
feasibility may be important arguments, but that there
is a need to reassess priorities and re-evaluate actions
to remedy the imbalance which exists in our societies.
Institutions must themselves be flexible in the face
of changing circumstance and institutions, which have
lost the ability to evaluate critically their purpose
and role may very well have lost sight of a clear
objective as well.

Illiteracy and innumeracy, serious as they are in a
society which demands competence in these areas as
pre-requisites for work and life, are only symbols of
people being cut off from the mainstream of life and

and denied participation in society. In our industrial societies, where great emphasis is placed on productivity, we feel that basic adult education should have priority over vocational training, chiefly because it is a necessary preparation for any type of vocational training and allows the individual to develop his own resources and become a productive member of society.

The working role is a vital one in social life: it gives dignity to the individual, direction to his social life and economic independence. It also contributes to society's welfare. When we look at people with inherited failure, we are looking at people who lack basic competence and social skills. We are conscious of the fact that such people are not readily employable, because they carry with them into working life the attitudes and lack of confidence which have become part of their existence. Inability to communicate at interviews, inflexibility in the workplace, aggressiveness towards supervisors and fellow-workers, absenteeism and lack of acceptance of responsibility do not develop in the workplace, but are symptoms of the individuals' insecurity and alienation from the objectives of society.

We believe that there are certain priorities in basic adult education. Some of these have already been emphasized by the European Community: migrant workers and ethnic minorities as well as young people in transition to work. But there are large groups of people who have been identified as suffering from multiple deprivation; there are the long-term unemployed, the elderly, people who are made redundant in middle-age or are forced into early

retirement. Many of these are left without any
constructive role in society and they urgently need
support and help either to keep them involved in the
mainstream of life or to enable them to participate
fully in society. Many people in backward rural
areas are particularly disadvantaged because of
their isolation and the lack of institutions
locally to help them to recognize and develop
their own resources.

We were unanimous that we in no way wished to belittle
vocational training when we emphasized the value of
basic adult education. Rather we are trying to
bridge the gaps that exist between vocational
training, particularly in a rigid traditional
sense, and education for life. We are aware of the
gradual changes occurring in the field of vocational
training and we praise CEDEFOP's efforts to
accelerate this process. In a time of rapid social
change it is important to use all the resources
of society to help people adapt. Vocational
training must take on many more aspects of
enlightened basic adult education, developing
peoples' competencies and motivation and helping
them to understand the approach to employment and
the work situation.

This is particularly important in situations of very
abrupt change, as in redundancy or in retirement,
People who have control of their own life situations,
who are used to taking responsibility and making
decisions, are much more likely to approach
situations of change in a positive manner. Those

who have remained in a state of dependency all their lives are likely to accept such changes as blows of fate and take on the role of chronically unemployed instead of seeking retraining or a new productive role.

This is particularly important in these times when there is much change in work structures due to micro-technology and other developments. Whatever work structure develops, new terms have to be evolved, changes have to be faced, and people particularly the disadvantaged, have to be prepared for them.

Our group recognized the potential of basing adult education programmes on local groups and in local centres, using local culture as a means to learning, and development of programmes. This would facilitate access to all local people to these centres and would allow for a multiplicity of approaches, ranging from individual tuition through small groups to the use of mass-media in association with group work. To develop these centres on a sufficiently wide scale, it was felt that they needed support or back-up from regional resource centres, which would provide training and resources. In addition, it was regarded as essential that a network of information and exchange should be formed through which experiences could be shared and field-workers could exchange ideas.

Finally the group made five very concrete proposals:

(1) that the Commission should make an assessment of finances available to basic adult education and of the facilities available to it,

(2) that there should be no cost to basic adult education participants in order not to deter them,

(3) that there should be a reallocation of public funds to provide sufficient resources for basic adult education programmes. Within the education system, this would mean reallocating some funds now applied to higher education. It is not intended to siphon funds from the primary school system. An effort should be made to allocate funds from unemployment insurance to basic adult education of unemployed persons, and labour-market agencies should be asked to accept pre-vocational training as part of their role. The use of all public buildings, where suitable, for adult education, is seen as essential,

(4) Exterprises should be asked to include basic education in their training programmes and should get tax benefits to encourage them to do this. Paid educational leave, in particular, should be opened to include basic adult education. Workers should also get tax relief for attending adult education courses,

(5) A significant percentage of the funds of the European
    Social Fund should be assigned to basic adult
    education because of its importance as a
    prerequisite for vocational training. Funds
    should be given to Member States on this clear
    understanding.

6.2. Working group No 2

Report of
Group 2:   The role of continuing education and training
as a preparation for new forms of employment
and development

    Chairman: Mr F. Taiti
    Rapporteur: Mr A. Boutin

The rapporteur expressed his gratitude to the Commission of the European Communities and the European Centre for the Development of Vocational Training, represented by Ms Fogg and by Mr Roger Faist, Director, and Mr Michel Blachère respectively, for kindly having afforded him the opportunity to participate in the deliberations on which he was about to report.

He also extended thanks to Mr Fabio Taiti, Group Chairman, and all the members of the Group, whose expert contributions had permitted the formulation of a comprehensive series of general, practical recommendations.

Pointing out that in his report he could not aspire to do justice to the wealth of ideas expressed, the rapporteur requested in advance the indulgence of the group members who might justifiably feel that the report reflects only the general tenor of their contributions.

Discussion concerning the role of continuing education and training as a preparation for new forms of employment and development leads on to observation of actual situations where such preparation is in operation.

After having interpreted the context of this linkage between training, employment, and development, Group 2 turned their attention to a number of general observations.

The context of possible links between training and new forms of employment and development is characterized by economic, social, and cultural changes now taking place in Europe. As Fabio Taiti mentioned, the development model of an industrial, urbanized society based on large-scale industry, rapid growth, and a steady rise in income and consumption is no longer in line with reality. Small and medium enterprises are now playing an increasingly important role. Alongside traditional secondary and tertiary activities a 'submerged' system of exchange of goods and services is gradually taking form which provides, partially or completely, for the livelihood of a growing section of the population.

It is this group of the working population for whom the primary labour market has an insufficient supply of job vacancies. Indeed, as H. C. Jones, S. Williams, and H. Janne pointed out in their contributions, the spread of certain technologies limits the number of jobs available; examples would be informatics machinery, microprocessors, and advanced office machinery.

At this point in the proceedings, the Group turned their attention to specific aspects of the working document "Perspectives in continuing education and training in the European Community", in particular those underlining the importance of intersectoral policies and the elaboration of a new, qualitative concept of economic growth.

It also gave consideration to observations reported by Michel Blachère in connection with CEDEFOP research projects on vocational training and job creation. The most effective of such operations are those which are conceptualized with close reference to the individual and collective situations which the training-based development project seeks to influence.

The context within which there is a link between training and new forms of employment is in part characterized by the fact that traditional training structures which have gradually developed in response to primary labour market demand have become so rigid and so centralized that they can no longer adapt to the rapidly accelerating primary labour market demand for new innovative skills.

The fact that in periods of high unemployment the training structures cannot provide all the qualifications requested, offering often instead qualifications which are in low demand, has led decision-makers to assume that our societies are nursing an education system which is gradually hypertrophying.

Since experience has shown that certain continuing training procedures prepare very satisfactorily for new forms of employment and development, as the CEDEFOP publication 'Training and the creation of activities' clearly illustrates, this fact need no longer be substantiated.

Types of training which are well adapted to the primary labour market and which can lead to steady employment should be maintained and further improved.

It is also necessary to encourage opportunities open to training of contributing to the diversification and consequently the expansion of the primary labour market. At the same time training policies should take into account the development of the secondary labour market in the interest of improving the economic efficiency of this market and increasing the number of its firms and workers.

Within the framework of these perspectives Group 2 prepared four recommendations.

1. CONTINUING TRAINING AND NEW FORMS OF EMPLOYMENT

Throughout Europe work organization is evolving rapidly at working time, functional, and legal levels. This development involves such innovations as reduced weekly working hours (now under study), staggered working hours, part-time employment, sabbatical leave, improved working conditions, and modalities facilitating worker autonomy.

Continuing training must take into account and contribute to these changes in the interest of both employers and workers.

Types of training associated with in-firm training such as educational leave and alternance training should be given preference in recognition of the fact that non.
schemes of this nature render habitual procedures of work and training more flexible.

Continuing training should likewise be provided in sectors where the evolution of work appears to be unfavourable and conducive to an increase in occasional employment, interim employment, leisure-time employment, and illegal employment.

Experience has shown that the provision of appropriate training stabilizes such jobs and thus contributes to the growth of small and medium industry. Such training also helps to transform certain types of illegal employment into recognized employment on either a self-employed or wage-earning basis.

Interim employment, the development of which poses problems, can be utilized in certain cases for pedagogical purposes. It enables trainees, for example, to enter working life for more or less long periods.

2. TRAINING AND NEW ACTIVITIES

Continuing training contributes to the adoption of innovations in economic and social practice, and its role in this context should therefore be systematically expanded.

European countries should be encouraged to link continuing training with their economic policies relating to energy conservation, new forms of energy, recycling, environmental protection, and informatics development. Put more generally all measures which utilize continuing training as a function of applied research should be supported.

The concept of new activities flows over into the field of technological innovation.

Continuing training should likewise encourage the development of services such as the personalized care of elderly persons in their own home and the reintegration of disabled persons into working life, services which are not only humane and efficacious but also create employment. They are at the same time more economical, since they eliminate the need for heavy investments.

Continuing training should also contribute to the satisfaction of needs which are not covered by the labour market or the public sector. New activities in the public sector which can be effectively promoted by continuing training should be sited in the publicly financed sector of associations and cooperatives and linked supportively to weak administrative structures.

3. SELECTION OF DEVELOPMENT TRAINING PROJECTS ON A GEOGRAPHICAL BASIS

This intersectorial approach has been shown to be very effective.

Development training projects, which utilize information, guidance, and training as functions serving to encourage the voluntary participation of social and cultural actors of a specific geographical zone in ongoing development efforts, should be supported.

A list, by no means complete, of objectives for which such projects could coordinate personal initiatives (some of which are relevant to the first two recommendations) follows:

- pretraining,
- development of new forms of work and new activities,
- polyactivities,
- creation of firms and cooperatives,
- growth in exchanges,
- economic and social animation,
- training for higher-level personnel of trade union organizations, local public organizations, consumer associations, etc.

4. FINANCING AND OPERATIONAL MEANS

The objectives defined in the first three recommendations can be attained only if the European countries are willing to provide more funds for continuing training, with expenditures being very carefully monitored.

In support of this general observation attention should be drawn to the direct and indirect costs of unemployment; they are such that the economic soundness of training preparing for new forms of employment and development is incontestable, quite apart from humane and cultural considerations.

Consequently, it appears desirable to

(1) continue unemployment benefits for job-seekers undergoing training;

(2) support the utilization of traditional education systems for continuing training purposes;

(3) encourage the integration of training programmes into economic, social, and cultural measures with which they are functionally linked;

(4) research possibilities of the financial participation of firms in projects which may be of interest to them;

(5) develop, in view of the fact that they are economical, self-training skills, utilizing the already tested procedures of sensitivity training and animation.

RECOMMENDATIONS CONCERNING RESEARCH AND STUDY PROJECTS

A. General recommendations

1. All those responsible for and engaged in continuing education and training at regional and local level should be informed of research and publications on the various experiences gained in Europe.
Contact and exchange among these persons should be facilitated by establishing a participative inter-project network permitting comparative evaluation.

2. A more flexible form should be given to the regulation which denies pilot project status and corresponding support from the European Social Fund to projects similar to an already assisted project.

3. The designation "Major educational development project" should be introduced, with specific assistance being granted to such projects.

4. Interest should be generated in the countries about to accede to the Community in devising education and training projects involving all the administrative sectors.

5. A proposal should be made to launch, at European level, a number of intersectoral study projects, their programming having been elaborated in consultation with the various irectorates concerned.

B. Continuing education and training and new forms of employment

1. A study should be made of the relation, as currently discernible in Europe, between the new forms of employment defined in the first recommendation and continuing education and training.

2. The European experience of educational leave should be reviewed.

3. A study should be made of the concepts of "key qualification" and "cumulative training unit" in connection with the restructuring of working hours and the rapid increase in autonomous work forms.

C. Education and training and new activities

1. The study on "Role of training in setting up new economic and social activities" which at present pertains to Italy, the United Kingdom and France, should be expanded to cover all EC Member States.

2. A study should be conducted on the medium and long-term possibilities for secondary and tertiary decentralization opened up by the development of informatics.

3. An examination should be undertaken of the new social roles to be accorded to specific categories of job-seeker and senior citizens.

4. A study covering all EC Member States should be conducted on new energy sources, energy conservation and waste recycling, pointing out the implications for continuing education and training.

D. Selection of development education and training projects on a geographical basis

1. Field studies should be undertaken in order to define the notions of "habitat and employment poles" and "education and training poles".

2. The various formulas used for training local development agents should be subjected to a comparative examination.

E. Financing and operational means

1. Evaluation criteria should be defined which are applicable to all projects.

2. The direct and indirect cost of unemployment should be calculated and the correlative profitability of education and training measures preparing for new forms of employment or activity evaluated.

3. A comparative evaluation should be undertaken of the costs of integrated education and training development projects and development schemes funded from multiple sources.

4. The costs of the various forms of self-education and training should be evaluated.

5. A study should be conducted in all EC Member States on the cost of allocating initial education funds for continuing education and training purposes.

André Boutin

6.3. Working group No 3

Report of

Group 3: The problems of older workers and the transition to retirement, and their implications for continuing education and training

Chairman: Prof. D. James
Rapporteur: Prof. C. Javeau

1. The Group commenced their work in a context of conflicting opinions, with the statements made by the various members initially reflecting a number of dichotomies. One area of divergence concerned the question whether a theoretical or pragmatic approach should be adopted in examining the topic under consideration. However, it was soon agreed that the introductory report served - as had indeed been the intention of its author - as a theoretical point of departure and general intellectual framework for the ensuing discussions and that these latter were to have a primarily practical orientation.

The other area of divergence distinguished the advocates of a normative approach complying with the existing framework of institutions and ideologies from those of an approach which could be described as a break with the past in so far as it takes into consideration the resistance often forthcoming from individuals when called upon by the above institutions to normalize their attitudes and behaviour patterns. This resistance can be traced back to escapist ideals and generally repressed inclinations to create new behaviour patterns, and its significance for evaluating

impending or long-term social innovations is great. Some
of these lines of resistance, in particular with regard to
employment and retirement, two concepts more or less
rejected by some, have aleady attained a statistical
dimension. They operate against education processes aiming
exclusively at socialization on the basis of artificially
imposed values. The Group acknowledged the existence of such
lines of resistance and the importance of drawing the
attention of decision-makers to the alternative forms of
life-style they imply and emphasizing the necessity of being
able to reflect in depth on isssues which are often
prematurely rejected as untouchable.

2. The interest shown in transition from work to retirement
stems from the following considerations:

a) In a democratic society such as the European Community
wishes to promote, older people have the right to be
treated in accordance with the rights of physical and social
integration, participation in community affairs, and
access without cost to citizen activities.

b) Adequate management of the physical and mental health
problems of the elderly is essential to their well-being.

c) Retirement from working life in accordance with varying
practices as described in the opening report does not imply
that the retirees are then shut out from the entire system
of activities which may or may not have a beneficial,
social feedback effect.

3. It is generally admitted that the sudden changeover from work to retirement, if not prepared for, can be a very traumatic experience indeed. In order to facilitate this transition one can

a) introduce flexible practices such as progressive retirement and partial retirement, dealt with in Document COM(80) 393 of the Commission of the European Communities entitled: 'Community guidelines on flexible retirement';

b) launch concurrently various initiatives preparing for retirement which are coupled with a process of adult education geared specifically to retirement and integrated into a broader policy of continuing training.

4. With regard to this educational preparation for retirement and indeed to all educational processes, the following questions are of primary importance:

a) What type of individual is this adult education expected to produce?
One could reply that a retiree who has been prepared for retirement should be an autonomous person who, having overcome the shock of retirement, is able to assume a new social role within the local community and the society at large.

b) What should this type of education aim at?
One could reply that it should aim at awakening in retirees curiosity for areas of activity or reflection which they had not explored during working life, fostering their interest in participating in community affairs and helping to meet community needs, strengthening their ability to get along with others, enabling them to properly manage their mental and physical health problems, etc.

c) What benefit does society and the community derive from this education?
Society in the large sense and the community in the narrow sense (to refer to the distinction drawn by de Tönnies between **Gesellschaft** and **Gemeinschaft**) are interested in welcoming into their midst senior citizens of good physical and mental health who can manage their own leisure time and who are capable of assuming new social roles in the interest of the common weal.

5. The group sought to draw a distinction between short-term and long-term continuing education measures preparing for retirement. Short-term measures are for the most part <u>adaptive</u> in nature and can be implemented in response to emergency situations (<u>first aid</u>) within the context of post-work educational processes, which latter should be reproached for not giving such situations adequate attention.
Adaptive measures primarily seek to permit the future retiree to

a) master the various personal problems which are bound to arise with the increase in leisure time: relations with close family members and other retirees, management of leisure time, etc.;

b) cope with the various demands placed on him by the social environment, such as those emerging from relations with local and national authorities, retiree associations, continuing education groups, etc. These measures necessarily include some elements of assistance; however, they are designed to eliminate or minimize retiree dependence on existing assistance institutions. They include not only elements of education in the narrow sense of the term but also aspects of _guidance_ and _counselling_.

6. Long-term measures are primarily _transformative_ in character and are based on the following considerations:

a) The economic crisis leads to the premature retirement of a body of workers who would otherwise continue to constitute an effective and useful work force. There is thus great waste of human resources, with many of the social needs of retirees being very poorly met, if at all.

b) With regard to health benefits, the same could be said of a large number of persons who retire at the "normal" age.

c) Legal provisions governing retirement and retirement pensions render difficult, especially in Member States of the Community, the launching of cooperative-form initiatives aimed at avoiding this waste of human resources.

The purpose of these short-term and long-term measures is to integrate unused human resources into various activities which bring social benefit. It is not a question of some retirees re-entering working life at a lower level of income but rather of designing and launching measures aimed at placing the rich potential of experience and competence of this target group at the disposal of various demand groups of the community, including the retirees themselves.

7. The Group stressed that whereas preparation for retirement should take into account specific needs, particularly preparation via measures of adaptation, educational activities should be integrated into a continuing education process comprising both pre-retirement educational processes (general education, vocational training, etc.) and adult education addressed to retirees.

Certain principles governing preparation for retirement can likewise be applied to measures aimed at other target groups located on the margin of economic life such as unemployed persons, juveniles and young adults, unemployed women, etc. Measures of transformation should be rooted in a long process of education fostering social creativeness and the ability to assume responsibility.

8. At the close of their deliberations the Group elaborated the following recommendations:

a) If under educational aspects preparation for retirement constitutes part of continuing education, preparation should continue after retirement and deal with the technical and legal aspects and likewise with the psychological and sociological aspects of retirement. School curricula should have room for a correct and socially accountable evaluation of retirement problems just as they have room for problems of employment and unemployment.

b) Encouraged by directives issued by the European Community, the Member States can facilitate measures of transformation aimed at the target group of retirees by modifying legal regulations governing retirement and retirement fund management and providing easier access to certain material resources such as public premises, legal documents, etc. The social partners should be encouraged to participate in this effort to facilitate transition from working life to retirement.

c) The development of voluntary activities, the role of which in educational measures preparing for retirement could be considerable, should be encouraged at local level. Voluntary activities can evolve from the initiative of retirees themselves; these initiatives should benefit from the provision of guidance and legal counselling, thus enabling retirees to play a useful role within the framework of measures of transformation.

This encouragement should not signify for public authority reasoning that these authorities may renounce their responsibilities in this respect. The decentralization process should take place under their supervision and with their guarantee and they should remain in a position to fulfil the compensatory functions which the various categories of retirees – for this is indeed not a homogeneous group – are entitled to expect of them.

d) The utilization within the framework of decentralization of available resources, above all material resources (schools, public buildings, homes, youth centres, etc.), should be facilitated via appropriate legislation at local level.

Efforts should furthermore be made to devise a better key for distributing the funds made available for education over all the elements of the education process, in particular by promoting the spatial and temporal integration of the various categories seeking education.

e) Support should be given to the launching of programmes designed by various Member States and interested local institutions on a joint basis, and aimed at the training of educators who will then concern themselves with the successive phases of continuing education, above all preparation for retirement. The services of the European Community should encourage at plurinational level the exchange of experiences gained at local level.

f) All research activities, which have intersectorial and/or plurinational bases of action, should be greatly encouraged, and the broad dissemination of the results of these activities should be effectively supported.

Annexes

A Seminar programme

ANNEX A

PROGRAMME

Tuesday, 14 October 1980

12.00   Arrival and registration of participants
CEDEFOP, Bundesallee 22, Berlin 15

14.30   Plenary introductory session

Introduction by the Chairman — Hywel C. Jones, Head of Division in Directorate General XII (Research, Science and Education) of the Commission of the European Communities

Welcoming address — Roger Faist, Director of CEDEFOP

Keynote speech — Shirley Williams, Research Fellow, Policy Studies Institute - London

General discussion — opened by Henri Janne, Président du Collège Scientifique, Institut de Sociologie, Université Libre de Bruxelles

Wednesday, 15 October 1980

09.30 - 12.30	Plenary session - selected themes for development
Chairman	George Wedell - Head of Division for Community action in Employment and Vocational Training (DG V), EC Commission
Introductory reports	1. The development of basic adult education and literacy. Eoin Murphy, Director, Dublin Institute for Adult Education
	2. Continuing education and training as a preparation for new forms of work and development. André Boutin, délégué régional à la formation professionnelle, Rhône-Alpes
	3. Older workers and the transition to retirement: implications for continuing education and training Claude Javeau, Professeur, Université Libre de Bruxelles
General discussion	
14.30-17.30	Working groups on selected themes
Group 1:	Chairman: Cornelius Snijders, Secretary General of the Open School Committee in the Netherlands
Group 2:	Chairman: Fabio Taiti, Director of the Centro Studi Investimenti Sociali, Rome
Group 3:	Chairman: David James, Director of the Department of Adult Education, University of Surrey - Guildford
19.00	Reception for the participants offered by the Senate of Berlin

Thursday, 16 October 1980

09.00-12.00 Working groups
Continuation of work

14.30-17.30 Working groups
Continuation and end of work

Friday, 17 October 1980

13.00-16.00 Concluding plenary session

Chairman Roger Faist

Keynote speech Continuing education and training: the contribution of the European Community
Jacques Delors, Director of the Centre de Recherche "Travail et Société", Université de Paris IX Dauphine

Discussion

Recommendations arising from working groups Eoin Murphy
André Boutin
Claude Javeau

Discussion

Closing address Olaf Sund, Senator for Employment and Social Affairs, Berlin

B List of participants

ANNEX B

LIST OF PARTICIPANTS

M. ADAMS	CEDEFOP
R. ALT	CEPFAR 25 rue de la Science B - 1040 Bruxelles
M. BARBARY	Directeur de la Formation AFPA 13, place de Villiers F-93100 Montreuil
Mrs. BASTRUP-BIRK	Commission des Communautés européennes UPB 04/12 XII/A/1 200, rue de la Loi B-1049 Bruxelles
M. BLACHERE	CEDEFOP
M. BOUCHET	Union des Cadres et Ingénieurs CGT-FO 2, rue de la Michodière F-75002 Paris
A. BOUTIN	Délégué Régional à la Formation Professionnelle Préfecture de la Région Rhône-Alpes Cours de la Liberté F- 69269 Lyon Cedex 1
G. CATELLI	Università Cattolica del S. Cuore Facoltà di Agricoltura I-29100 Piacenza
A. COLEMAN	The Pre-Retirement Association of Great Britain and Northern Ireland 19 Udine Str. - Tooting GB-London SW17 8PP
J. DELORS	Directeur Centre de Recherche "Travail et Société" Université de Paris IX Dauphine Place du Maréchal de Lattre de Tassigny F-75116 Paris

D. DENORRE	Conseiller Fédération des Entreprises de Belgique 4, rue Ravenstein B-1000 Bruxelles
L. DUBOIS	Coordinateur de la Formation Professionnelle pour le Hainaut Centre Polyvalent de Formation Professionnelle de l'ONEM Quai de Brabant B-6000 Charleroi
P. DUNNE	ANCO - The Industrial Training Authority 27-33 Baggot Court IRL-Dublin 4
R. FAIST	CEDEFOP
M. FAULKNER	Commission des Communautés européennes A-1 01/20 DG V 200, rue de la Loi B-1049 Bruxelles
Mrs K. FOGG	Commission des Communautés européennes UPB 04/12 XII/A/1 200, rue de la Loi B-1049 Bruxelles
Mrs H. FOSTER	BIBB 3, Fehrbelliner Platz D-1000 Berlin 31
D. GUERRA	CEDEFOP
H.N. HEINEMANN	4, Burbery Lane Great Neck New York, NY 11023, USA
P.H. HUGENHOLTZ	Federatie Nederlandse Vakbeweging Postbus 8456 Plein '40'-45 nr. 1 NL-Amsterdam

H.D. HUGHES	Crossways Mill Street - Islip GB-Oxford OX5 2SZ
Mrs N.E. McINTOSH	The Open University The Centre for International Cooperation and Services Walton Hall GB- Milton Keynes MK7 6AA
J.P. JALLADE	Fellow of the Institute of Education of the European Cultural Foundation Université de Paris IX Dauphine Place du Maréchal de Lattre de Tassigny F-75116 Paris
D. JAMES	Department of Adult Education University of Surrey Guildford GB- Surrey GU2 5XH
H. JANNE	Université de Bruxelles Institut de Sociologie 244, avenue Louise - Bte 13 B-1050 Bruxelles
C. JAVEAU	1, avenue du Geal B-1170 Bruxelles
H.C. JONES	Commission des Communautés européennes UPB 04/22 XII/A/1 200, rue de la Loi B-1049 Bruxelles
W. KIRZ	Senator für Schulwesen Abt. III (Weiterbildung) Stresemannstr. 72 D-1000 Berlin 61
F. KJARUN	Projektleder Skolevangen 7 Benløse - Ringsted DK-Islandsbrygge

A. KOELINK	Directeur generaal voor het voortgezed onderwijs Ministerie van onderwijs en wetenschappen Nieuwe Uitleg 1 NL-Den Haag
J. KUHL	Institut für Arbeitsmarkt und Berufsforschung Regensburger Str. 104 D-8500 Nürnberg
Miss A. LEWIS	Manpower Services Commission 95, Wigmore Street GB-London W1
P. MAKEHAM	Department of Employment Caxton House Tothill Street GB-London SW1
H. MARCANTONIS	Université d'Athènes Zonarastr. 1 GR-Athen 708
H.M. MULLER	Arbeitskreis Orientierungs- und Bildungshilfe e V Jahnstr. 13 D-1000 Berlin 61
Father Eoin MURPHY	Dublin Institute of Adult Education 1-3 Mountjoy Square IRL-Dublin 1
M. MURPHY	AONTAS National Association of Adult Education 14, Fitzwilliam Place IRL-Dublin 2
T. O'CONNOR	Research Director The Retirement Planning Council of Ireland Boylan Community Centre Sussex Street IRL-Dun Laoghaire - Co Dublin

Frau M. OELS	VHS Berlin-Charlottenburg Heerstr. 12/14 D-1000 Berlin
M.L. OSWALD	Hasenheide 19 D-1000 Berlin 61
J.M. OUAZAN	Institut Travail et Société Université de Paris IX Dauphine Place du Maréchal de Lattre de Tassigny F-75116 Paris
K.V. PANKHURST	OECD Directorate for Social Affairs Manpower and Education 2, rue André Pascal F-75775 Paris Cedex 16
B. PASQUIER	BIT . Programme des Nations-Unies pour le Développement Casier des Nations-Unies Rabat-Chellah - Maroc
J. PERQUY	Algemeen Christelijk Vakverbonds Vormingsdienst 121, rue de la Loi B-1000 Bruxelles
L. PESCIA	Istituto per la Ricostruzione - IRI 89, via Vittorio Veneto I-Roma
R. PINARD	Directeur du Personnel Gilette France 99, avenue de Genève F-74010 Annecy
C. PONCET	Directeur Centre INFFO Tour Europe - Cedex 07 F-92080 Paris-La Défense

P.M. REGUZZONI S.J.	Centro Studi Sociali "Aggiornamenti sociali" Piazza S. Fedele, 4 I-20121 Milano
W. ROTHWEILER	D.G.B. Hans-Bückler Str. 39 D-4000 Düsseldorf 1
V. SABA	Fondazione Giulio Pastore Via della Fontanella di Borghese 35 I-00186 Roma
J.J. SCHEFFKNECHT	ADEP Tour Franklin - Cedex 11 F-92081 Paris-La Défense
M. RICK	B.IBB 3, Fehrbelliner Platz D-1000 Berlin 31
B. SCHWARTZ	326, rue Saint Jacques F-75015 Paris
J. SNELL	29, rue d'Ahlerange L-Esch-sur-Alzette
C.J. SNIJDERS	Commissie Open School Onderwijscentrum Zeist Laan van Vollenhove 3227 NL-3706 AR Zeist
C. STAPEL	Secretary Folk High School Association Guardini-Nes 8 NL-Bergen N.H.
F. TAITI	Direttore CENSIS Centro Studi Investimenti Sociali Piazza di Novella 2 I-00199 Roma

M. THIVAUD	Association des Ages 9, rue de Vauvilliers F-75001 Paris
Herr TILLMANN	BIBB 3, Fehrbelliner Platz D-1000 Berlin 31
J.P. TITZ	Division for Adult Education and Permanent Education Directorate for Education Culture and Sport Council of Europe F-67000 Strasbourg
M. P. SKYUM-NIELSEN	Dansk Arbejdsgivertorening Vester Volgade 113 DK-1552 København
E. VERCELLINO	CGIL Corso d'Italia, 25 I-00100 Roma
L. VERSWIJVEL	Comité belge pour les relations internationales de la jeunesse Place Madou, 6 B-1030 Bruxelles
D. WATKINS	Manchester Business School Booth Street West GB-Manchester M15 5PB
A. WATTS	National Institute for Careers Education and Counselling Bateman Street GB - Cambridge CB2 1LZ
G. WEDELL	Commission des Communautés européennes A-1 01/17 200, rue de la Loi B-1049 Bruxelles

Mrs S. WILLIAMS   Policy Studies Institute
                       1-2 Castle Lane
                       GB-London SW1E 6DR

M. BOESPFLUG   Mouvement International ATD
                       Quart Monde
                       107, avenue du Général Leclerc
                       F-95480 Pierrelaye

N. WOLLSCHLÄGER   CEDEFOP

+++

C
List of papers prepared on specific aspects of the three seminar themes

Annex C

Papers prepared on specific aspects of the three seminar themes

THEME 1: The development of basic adult education and literacy

1.1 Educational disadvantage and the adult learner
Father Eoin Murphy, Director of the Dublin Institute for Adult Education, Ireland

1.2 Integrated methods for basic adult education programmes - some important issues
Mr Anthony R. Kaye, Senior Lecturer in Educational Technology, Open University, United Kingdom

1.3 Report on the problems of the acquisition of literacy in an enlarged Community
Ms Anna Lorenzetto, Professore Ordinario Educazione degli Adulti, Facoltà di Magistero dell'Università di Roma, Italy

THEME 2: The role of continuing education and training as a preparation for new forms of employment and development.

2.1 Continuing education and training in preparation for new types of work and social development
Mr André Boutin, délégué régional à la formation professionnelle, Lyon, France

2.2   Vocational training in the face of the challenge of regional development
      Mr Fabio Taiti, Director, CENSIS, Rome, Italy

2.3   Continuing training in the face of new forms of work and development
      Mr Michel Blachère, CEDEFOP, Berlin

THEME 3 : The problems of older workers and the transition to retirement, and their implications for continuing education and training

3.1   Old age and retirement
      Professor Claude Javeau, Université Libre de Bruxelles, Belgium

3.2   Older workers and the transition to retirement
      Mr. Michael J. Faulkner, expert detached from the United Kingdom Department of Employment working with the Commission's services

CEDEFOP — European Centre for the Development of Vocational Training

New perspectives in continuing education and training in the European Community — Seminar report

Luxembourg : Office for Official Publications of the European Communities

1983 — 180 pp. — 16 × 20 cm

DE, EN, FR, IT

ISBN 92-825-3535-5

Catalogue number : HX-32-81-956-EN-C

Price (excluding VAT) in Luxembourg
ECU 4   BFR 180   IRL 2.70   UKL 2.40   USD 4